AT YOUR SERVICE:

A HANDS-ON GUIDE TO THE PROFESSIONAL DINING ROOM

AT YOUR SERVICE:
A HANDS-ON GUIDE TO THE PROFESSIONAL DINING ROOM

THE CULINARY INSTITUTE OF AMERICA | JOHN W. FISCHER

WILEY

John Wiley & Sons, Inc.

Published by John Wiley & Sons, Inc., Hoboken, New Jersey
Published simultaneously in Canada

For general information about our other products and services, please contact our Customer Care Department within the United States at (800) 762-2974, outside the United States at (317) 572-3993 or fax (317) 572-4002.

Wiley also publishes its books in a variety of electronic formats. Some content that appears in print may not be available in electronic books. For more information about Wiley products, visit our web site at www.wiley.com.

LIBRARY OF CONGRESS CATALOGING-IN-PUBLICATION DATA

At your service: a hands-on guide to the professional dining room.
    p. cm.
ISBN 0-764-55747-5 (cloth)
1. Food service. I. Culinary Institute of America.
TX943.A88 2005
647.95—dc22

                    2004030255

PRINTED IN THE UNITED STATES OF AMERICA

10 9 8 7 6 5 4 3 2 1

ACKNOWLEDGMENTS

This book is dedicated to the memory of Carmine Stanzione, who showed me that it is possible to be a teacher, restaurant manager, and gentleman simultaneously.

Thanks to everybody who helped to make this book a reality: Sue Cussen (thanks also for the title), copy editor Sue Warga, and my editor Lisa Lahey.

For the encouragement and additional support, I thank Dr. Kathy Zraly, Tom Peer, C.I.A. President Tim Ryan, and the entire staff and faculty of the Restaurant Operations group.

I would like to thank everyone I've worked with, because they all taught me something along the way. In particular, Waldy Malouf has been a true mentor and friend for most of those years. Also, Attilio Vosilla has been a great friend and co-manager in no less than three restaurants. . . . I just wish I had his hair.

Special thanks to my wife, Nathalie, who picked up wherever I left off when it was time for me to write. But mostly for her unwavering support and help during this project, and, of course, forever.

Finally, I wouldn't be doing what I do now were it not for my family. My late father, Robert Fischer, was responsible for my fledgling interest in wine. My mom, Mary Ellen, showed me how to be a great host and make it seem effortless. My brother Tom, sister Mary and I have been the staff for many parties at our homes-as hectic as it may be sometimes, we always have a great time. I use my family as the standard against which I measure restaurants. Believe me, it's a pretty high standard that only the best restaurants reach.

CONTENTS

CHAPTER 1:
THE BASICS OF
HOSPITALITY
AND SERVICE

SETTING: A formal French restaurant

THE PLAYERS: Four ladies from New York on a visit; the maître d'hôtel

The dinner guests had thoroughly enjoyed the food and wine and were pleased by the service, but they'd already missed the next-to-last train from Poughkeepsie to Manhattan, and the departure time of the last train was drawing close. As they paid their check, the maître d' phoned a local cab company to take the ladies to the train station. They left in a rush of thanks and well-wishing, hoping to catch their train.

The foursome had been the last customers for the evening, and the maître d' left soon thereafter. Pulling out of the parking lot, he saw the ladies still waiting and knew that if the cab didn't arrive that instant, they would miss the train. But no cab could be seen down the road. There was only one way to get the ladies to the train station on time, and so he squeezed them all into his rather small car and made a beeline for the station. The car was not built to accommodate that number of people, and each bump they hit brought a gale of laughter and references to who had eaten the most dessert. At the station, the guests scrambled out of the car, calling their thanks as they dashed into the nearest car of the train. He didn't hear from them again. He didn't need to.

Admittedly, this was a rather extreme circumstance, and one that is not likely to happen on a regular basis. However, it is possible to apply the same principle of hospitality almost every day. For example, guests are sometimes in a hurry to get to the theater and don't have time for dessert. I have known waiters who would pack up some cookies or petit fours and hand them to the guests as they rushed out the door. It's a simple, thoughtful action that takes little effort but shows true hospitality.

WHAT IS HOSPITALITY?

BECAUSE I TEACH HOSPITALITY, I spend a lot of time in class discussing the concept. The H-word is used a lot at the school—perhaps a bit too much: "We're in the hospitality business"; "Let's show the guests some of our famous hospitality." Despite such constant use of the term, students often arrive not knowing exactly what it means. And it's not all that easy to pin down: I can teach students the smallest details of fine table service, but the concept of hospitality extends beyond the mastery of such professional skills.

To help bring the concept to life, I begin with an example that draws upon the students' own memories and emotions. I ask them to recall an extra-special gather-

HOSPITALITY *(hospi'tæliti).*
[a. OF. hospitalité (12–13th c. in
Hatz-Darm.), ad. L. hospitalitas,
f. hospitalis (see HOSPITAL a.).] 1.
a. The act or practice of being
hospitable; the reception and
entertainment of guests,
visitors, or strangers, with
liberality and goodwill.
(Definition according to the
Oxford English Dictionary)

ing at their home—perhaps a holiday meal, friends from far away arriving for a joyous celebration, or Mom or Dad's boss coming over for dinner. Most of the students have experienced such an occasion. Then I ask them what their house was like for the couple of days beforehand. They recount stories of long shopping lists and the back of the car filled with groceries. Cleaning took on a new dimension, perhaps requiring the use of nontraditional implements such as toothbrushes and Q-Tips, and the scent of Lemon Pledge hung in the air. Martial law reigned in the kitchen as parents prepared dishes that weren't run-of-the-mill dinner fare. Then, the main event: taking guests' coats at the door, remembering what everyone wanted to drink, carefully carving the turkey and arranging the meat on an enormous platter, and each member of the family hustling around the house to make sure that none of the guests wanted for anything. Every activity pertained to making the guests feel comfortable and welcome. Recalling this, most students immediately understand, on an emotional level, what hospitality is all about.

The joy of planning and executing a terrific party, of being a great host and participating in your guests' delight, is one of the great pleasures in life. When students ask me what draws people into the restaurant business, this is what I tell them. And this, in fact, is the reason I teach hospitality for a living. What I learned in my family about treating guests well—especially from my mother, who is a master of the dinner party—is what spurred me onto this career path.

At its best, when everything comes together, running a dining room feels like you're giving the best dinner party ever. Trained cooks and a great chef send out delicious food; beautiful surroundings and the right music coax guests into an expansive mood; a professional, highly trained staff brings the guests whatever they need, ideally before they know they need it. In the dining room, we are presented with the opportunity to bring complete strangers into our warm, welcoming space and make them feel part of our family, so that they want to return over and over again.

So this is hospitality—inviting guests in and ensuring that we have done everything within our control to make them happy. This task is difficult enough for any person to carry out at home two or three times a year. The kicker is that we do it for a living every day. We are in the hospitality *business.* And making hospitality a business involves identifying those aspects of a fabulous special occasion at home that can and should be reproduced in the restaurant, and then reliably performing those actions whenever necessary.

HOUSE STYLE

EACH OF US HAS OUR OWN STYLE when it comes to taking care of guests in our homes, and the same is true of restaurants. One factor that goes into determining a restaurant's house style is the type of establishment: fine dining, with luxurious surroundings and a leisurely pace; bistro or trattoria, which encompasses a wide range of restaurants, all with a simple, cozy feel; or family-style or casual, which may range from diner to theme restaurant and beyond.

Another factor is the restaurant owner's personality. Just as some people may be huggers and others air-kissers, some restaurant owners prefer that the house style be a formal one, while others embrace a more casual feel. For instance, in a family-style Italian restaurant it might be appropriate for the owner or waiter to warmly greet a guest by his or her first name. However, in a high-end French restaurant, it is likely that the guest will be greeted more formally, with the maître d' or owner using a courtesy title and the guest's surname. There are, of course, many possible variations along this spectrum—for example, some formal places are more relaxed than others while still maintaining an elegant, polished feel.

A third element is the restaurant's intended clientele. Just as someone giving a dinner party at home would tailor the event to the guests—perhaps a catered white-glove dinner for members of a charity organization's board of directors, a taco buffet for families from the neighborhood—a restaurant proprietor has to decide what kind of establishment he or she wants to run and establish a style that matches. I've worked in formal restaurants where any waiter who touched his or her nose while in the dining room would be polishing silverware for a week. Conversely, I've also worked in a family-run Italian restaurant where there was lots of hugging and kissing. In each case, the house style was both appropriate to the guests and a reflection of the owner's personal style.

Not to be left out, the style of your restaurant can also determine which service model to use.

THE HISTORY OF SERVICE

BEFORE DISCUSSING the different types of service, it might help to know how service of food has evolved through the ages.

THE EARLY STAGES

Some of the earliest writings on serving food describe dining in Greek high society. There weren't many public dining places, so entertaining took place mostly in the home. Rather small rooms with couches for the guests were used for the purpose.

Food was brought out in large dishes from which the guests served themselves, tossing shells and bones onto a small table in front of them. As the courses progressed, the tables would be removed and quickly replaced with clean tables.

The Romans borrowed much from Greek culture and developed more of their own. Roman food was much more complex, with many more spices and seasonings. Exotic spices were, of course, a sign of affluence because most of them came from the Far East. Diners sat in places determined by status—places of honor being reserved for the host and important guests. The room they ate in was called a *triclinium*, with three benches in a U-shape. Each couch held three reclined guests who leaned on their left sides, leaving their right hand free to grasp food. Again, servants brought out food in a series of courses. The reclining thing sounds comfortable, but it probably wasn't too good for the digestion.

CATERINA DE' MEDICI is credited with bringing the fork into widespread use as a dining utensil. By using a fork to pick up bites of food, guests could keep their hands clean throughout the meal. This allowed use of finer napery, and even better table manners.

THE SIZE OF DINING ROOMS IN GREEK HOMES was referred to in terms of the number of couches within. "Yes, my husband Nikos and I are building a new house with a five-coucher!"

THE MIDDLE AGES AND THE RENAISSANCE

Anglo-Saxon banquets during medieval times were rather large affairs held in the main hall of a castle. The tables were in a large U, with the host and prominent guests seated at the head table. The tables were covered with a white cloth, and the salt cellar was placed in front of the most important person at the table—salt was highly valuable then. You could tell how important you were by how close the salt was to your place at the table. The food was served from large bowls on the table; guests brought their own knives for cutting food into serving pieces and would often share a plate among three or four diners. French banquets differed in that the tablecloth hung over the sides and was used by the diners to wipe off their hands and faces. How civilized!

French banquets became more and more lavish, with huge displays of food and decoration. Toward the end of the eighteenth century, only the aristocracy was eating this way . . . but not for long. The French Revolution in 1789 toppled the French monarchy and nobility, and left a lot of chefs unemployed. This was a major factor in the growth of restaurants—the chefs had to ply their trade as businesspeople. Restaurants had been in existence before the revolution, but the growth of the middle class created more demand for them.

As the fourteenth century ended, food service was becoming the subject of study and began to be respected. Taillevent (Guillaume Tirel) was cook to both Charles V and Charles VI, and he wrote the book *Le Viander,* which codified the cooking of the day.

However, the first signs of fine dining appeared in the sixteenth century in the court of the Medici family of Florence, Italy. The dissemination of fine dining habits began when Caterina de' Medici (1519–1589) married King Henri II of France and brought a phalanx of trained cooks, chefs, servants, and sommeliers with her. She also introduced the habits of fine dining to the French. Her cousin Marie de' Medici, as wife to Henri IV, took over where Caterina had left off. One of the most famous chefs of all time, François La Varenne, received his training in the kitchen of Henri IV, and he wrote a book in 1651 that looked to the future, *Le Cuisinier François* (François the Cook).

TYPES OF SERVICE

AMERICAN SERVICE, FRENCH SERVICE, RUSSIAN SERVICE, MONGOLIAN SERVICE: only one of them requires the use of yak pelts. The other three types of service (and a few additional ones) are used in professional dining rooms these days. The style of service that you choose depends on two things: the demeanor of the dining room and the demands of the situation. A formal restaurant is a more likely place for French service to be used, and having twelve people at a banquet table would be a good time to break out the platters for some Russian or butler service. While the basic tenets of each style are pretty well defined, there is some blurring of the lines between them—and some disagreement about which is which. In fact, while researching this subject I found Russian and French service described in the exact same words in the same book!

Below you will find some relatively simple explanations of the styles along with some advantages and disadvantages of each.

As the world moved into the Industrial Revolution in the 1800s, the world of food service moved quickly to fulfill the needs of workers. Factories drew large numbers of workers who had to be fed. The tight mealtime schedules caused a need for fast, efficient service. Counter service became popular, and the first Horn & Hardart Automat opened in Philadelphia in 1902. Fine dining wasn't dead, though. Delmonico's (opened in 1837) had a 100-page menu with 370 dishes and catered to New York's elite. In less than a century, fine food service went from being the province of the wealthy and powerful to being much more egalitarian and democratic. As Americans continue to seek out sources of prepared food, food service will become increasingly part of their lives.

AMERICAN SERVICE

This is a very popular style of service used not just in America but in many other countries. Its hallmark is efficiency, and thus it tends to be used in more casual and high-volume restaurants. Its efficiency has, though, attracted many purveyors of fine dining and led to its use in many formal restaurants.

In American service, the food is cooked and plated in the kitchen. The waiter delivers the food, one plate at a time, to the guests at the table, ladies first. These days, most service professionals agree that the guest should be served from the right side, with the waiter's right hand. Clearing of plates is also performed with the

ONE OF THE FIRST RESTAURANTS (as we think of them) was opened by A. B. Beauvilliers in 1782. It was La Grande Taverne de Londres, and it offered a true à la carte menu; until then, most dining establishments offered a fixed menu, or table d'hôte. The option to choose for themselves was obviously a great attraction for guests.

right hand from the right side. This goes against my earlier training, in which I was taught to serve from the left with the left, and clear from the right with the right. Whichever one you choose, train the staff to do so consistently. When the right hand is used for serving or clearing, the waiter should move around the table in a clockwise direction; it is more efficient (and safer) because the waiter is, by definition, walking forward rather than backing up. Conversely, any task performed with the left hand should lead the waiter around the table in a counterclockwise direction.

In most American restaurants, the service brigade consists of waiters, runners, and bussers. The waiter interacts directly with the guests and manages his or her station. Runners bring food from the kitchen into the dining room, and bussers clear and reset tables, pour water, refill bread, and assist the runner. Rather than three-person teams, most restaurants have more waiters than runners, and more runners than bussers. This is because the runners' and bussers' jobs are more general and can cover more territory in the restaurant—their work isn't as guest-specific.

FRENCH SERVICE

Originally, French service was used with meals that consisted of three courses, one of which was already set on the table when guests entered the room (hence the term *entrée*). Subsequent courses were brought into the room on silver platters and served from gueridons. Between courses, the guests would get up from the table and it would be cleared—not exactly a turn-and-burn.

While the current incarnation of French service is not quite as time-consuming as the original, this style has been relegated to the formal dining rooms of a few restaurants and hotels around the world. Not only does it require a large amount of expensive equipment, there is also the need for a highly trained service brigade to carry it out. This brigade is made up of the following personnel:

- **THE CAPTAIN** almost never leaves the dining room. He or she is always in sight of the guests and is their main contact. The captain takes most of the orders, prepares the tableside items, and runs the station with the assistance of the rest of the team. The captain must have a profound knowledge of food and wine and be able to translate that knowledge into language that is understandable to each and every guest. As a mixture of salesperson, confidant, and advocate, the captain is the most influential person with regard to the quality of the guest's dining experience.

- **THE FRONT WAITER** is the captain's lieutenant. His or her duties include regular table maintenance such as pouring water and clearing plates, as well as assisting the captain with tableside cooking and tending to the guests while the captain is occupied, either at the gueridon or at another table. Occasionally, the front waiter will take drink or dessert and coffee orders, but the dinner order (because of its importance and intricacy) is usually taken by the captain. The front waiter helps to coordinate the delivery of food to the table with the back waiter; the same team does most of the table clearing as well. The front waiter's position may not be as glamorous as that of the captain, but the captain relies heavily on the front waiter's efficacy.

- **THE BACK WAITER** is also sometimes called a runner, but the terms aren't exactly equivalent. A runner is someone who brings food from the kitchen anywhere in the dining room. A back waiter, though, is part of a team that is responsible for a specific set of tables and brings food from the kitchen to those tables. In addition to running food, the back waiter will assist the front waiter as needed, perhaps pouring water, serving bread, clearing tables, and the like. So a true back waiter does more than just run food; he or she is responsible to the service team.

- **BUSSER** or **GUARD** is a position that some people, unfortunately, look down upon. Needless to say, the busser is an extremely valuable member of the service team and can be integral to that team's success. Primary responsibilities include basic table maintenance (bread and water), clearing, and the resetting of recently vacated tables. A great busser can lighten the burden on the rest of the service team, enabling them to concentrate more on serving the guests.

In French service the various staffers have to work as a team. Each member has both primary responsibilities and secondary responsibilities—for example, the captain will sometimes pour water when the front waiter is helping the back waiter deliver food to a table. The captain, though, should not be running food from the kitchen to the dining room unless the situation is dire. I remember being chided by Waldy Malouf for going into the kitchen when I, as a captain, should have been in the dining room: "How do you know if they need something if you're standing in here?" Waldy, of course, was right.

The hierarchy of the classic service team works very well, but there are limitations. First of all, the restaurant has to be big enough that four-person teams can fit in the dining room. Second, the prices have to be high enough that all the members of a four-person team can make enough money to live on. Lastly, it has to fit with the demeanor of the dining room—you'll probably never hear "Welcome to Charlie's Chili Bungalow. I'm Jean-Pierre and I will be your captain this evening." In the right place, though, a well-trained, experienced team can be a joy to watch at work.

RUSSIAN OR PLATTER SERVICE

Definitions of Russian service vary, but the most common involves platters of food being prepared in the kitchen and brought to the table, with the server placing the food on the guest's plate from the left side with the right hand. Sauce and garnish are served either by that waiter or by another one following right behind.

Advantages of this model include the relatively quick and personal service of hot food to a large number of guests. It also shows off the abilities of the service staff with relatively simple training. One disadvantage is that servers have to learn how to use the service spoon and fork in combination as a sort of tongs. Also, by the time the waiter gets to the last guest at the table, the platter can start looking a bit ragged. Portion control can be a bit tricky, especially if a guest asks for additional food, leaving the waiter without enough food for everyone at the table. This rarely happens, though, so the other two potential problems loom a bit larger.

These days, it is rather common for waiters in many types of dining rooms to use Russian service to place bread on guests' plates. Additionally, being handy with serviceware can be helpful when splitting menu items onto two plates for guests, either on the gueridon, on the side stand, or at the table. While it might take a bit of practice, the effort will pay off, at least in the form of confidence at the table.

BUTLER SERVICE

Take Russian service and let the guests serve themselves from the platter. That's butler service. The service utensils are on the platter for the guest to use, and the waiter still walks around the table counterclockwise, serving to the guests' left side (starting with the lady to the host's left).

ENGLISH SERVICE

This is a style of service that I have never seen in use before, but I am still fascinated by the idea of it. Essentially, it is Thanksgiving dinner in a restaurant. The food is fully cooked in the kitchen and sent out on platters to the dining room. The host carves the meat or plates the main course and hands the plates to the guests, who pass the plates around the table. Side dishes are sent out for the guests to help themselves, but the wait staff performs the other aspects of table maintenance. It would be used in a country club or some other venue where the guest wanted to mimic a home-style setting while still being waited on.

FAMILY SERVICE

Family-style service is quite popular in some value-oriented restaurants, and also in places where the style fits with the theme. For instance, some Italian restaurants feature large platters of food that are brought to the table, where the guests serve themselves onto empty extra plates. It is a remarkably efficient style of service that can make a lot of sense (and money) for you in the right situation. The waiter's job is made easier in a number of ways: the order is easier to take, the food is easier to deliver, and individuals largely take care of themselves. The kitchen is also helped by the fact that a table of four can be served with three large platters of food instead of four appetizers and four main courses—three large plates of food take much less time to prepare than eight single servings.

Family-style service can be used in other types of casual restaurants. If it is appropriate to the demeanor of the restaurant, I highly recommend giving it a shot. Customers enjoy the chance to serve themselves, it can lighten the burden in both the dining room and kitchen, and it can lower labor costs.

As you can see, house style can function in two ways—both as a marketing tool, to attract a certain type of clientele (for example, businesspeople, or teens out with their friends), and as a way of creating regular business, by enticing back people who feel comfortable there.

THE BUSINESS END

TO BE SUCCESSFUL, any business must establish and maintain a consistent level of quality. On any given night, customers should be able to walk into a restaurant and experience the type of hospitality the restaurant has established a reputation for. In the restaurant business, as in any field from sports to media to manufacturing, reliability and consistency are achieved through training and practice. To take a very different example, in basketball a winning team will always have more than one player who can be counted on to score free throws consistently, especially when the game is on the line, and that sort of consistency is due almost exclusively to hard work and practice between games. In the restaurant business, a successful restaurant has a trained staff who not only can manage an average night in a way that keeps customers satisfied but also can handle just about anything that's thrown their way, such as a large last-minute party with many special requests on a busy night, an equipment malfunction in the kitchen, even a waiter suddenly becoming ill and other staff having to pitch in to cover his or her tables.

Occasional flashes of brilliance are all well and good, perhaps drawing a lot of attention from food critics, but making quality a habit—establishing a routine so that every guest is greeted warmly within thirty seconds of entering the restaurant, giving waiters the information they need about the food so that guests' questions about the menu can be answered on the spot, making sure the dining room illumination and temperature are always at specified levels—is what brings customers back.

THE DIFFERENCE BETWEEN HOSPITALITY AND SERVICE

WHILE, AS WE HAVE SEEN, hospitality is a concept that depends on feelings and impressions, the essence of service resides in action. Service is being able to carry four dinner plates without spilling the sauce, or opening a bottle of Champagne without spewing foam onto the floor. Restaurateurs do these things to make people feel comfortable and attended to. While the tasks themselves do not involve emotion, they enable it, in the sense that carrying them out in a professional manner evokes positive feelings in guests.

Satisfying the instinctual need to take nourishment is the reason people eat. But why do they go to a restaurant to do so when good food is so widely available and can so easily be prepared at home? With over half of Americans' meals originating outside the home today, that is no trivial question. There are many factors that contribute to the rise in dining out, such as increasingly busy schedules, greater mobility, and larger amounts of disposable income, but a primary answer is that dining out feels good: nice people bring you delicious things to eat and drink, and then wash the dishes after you leave. Restaurant folks take care of you. If hospitality is the final destination, service is the road map and the car.

IS HOSPITALITY TRAINABLE?   CAN RESTAURANT STAFF
be trained to provide good service? Yes. But the first step is to identify exactly what good service means in a particular restaurant setting.

The first step is to identify what feelings and experiences you want a guest in your establishment to have, and then determine what specific actions on the part of the staff will help to bring them about. Let me use an example from a home dinner party to show what I mean here.

A friend had invited a number of interesting people to dinner and spared no expense with regard to food and drink. Yet somehow the evening just didn't come together. None of the guests had ever met before that night, and the awkward silences were amplified by the absence of background music. While the food was of very high quality, the various menu items were all very complicated and difficult to eat, and they did not complement each other well. The guests were left on their own to rummage through the fridge for any beverage other than water. Every minute felt like an hour, and many guests seemed vaguely ill at ease. As the evening progressed, I compiled a mental checklist of a few changes that would have made this a much more pleasurable evening for everyone (though I never did relay that list to my friend, mostly because I didn't want to hurt her feelings). Some quiet jazz on the stereo, a simple bar with some wine and mineral water, and a few changes to the

menu would have enhanced the experience, making for a more relaxed, convivial atmosphere that would have encouraged us all to get to know each other.

This, of course, was a home dinner party, but the lessons apply to the restaurant business as well. Specific actions can lead to desired feelings and emotions on the guest's part, and these actions can be singled out, defined, described, and put into simple, trainable terms—for example, anticipating the pace of a meal and bringing successive courses at just the right time, making suggestions of menu items that will complement dishes already ordered, and presenting the check at just

WALDY MALOUF, chef/partner at Beacon Restaurant, New York, notes:

"Is hospitality teachable? Yes, but it's difficult. You can train it when someone doesn't understand the fulfillment that they can get out of being hospitable. Sometimes there's a preconceived attitude, when [the staff members] just haven't experienced the pleasures of providing pleasure. And if you show them that and they start to experience it, then it's teachable. I mean, a lot of times people have a preconceived notion that they're just going to be a slave, thinking they're not going to like waiting on people. But if you show them through training and creating a pleasurable workplace, and maintaining a level of professionalism where the level of respect is equal from the customer to the staff and vice versa, you can show them that being hospitable feels good."

Another perspective comes from **ANTHONY SCOTTO JR.,** proprietor of Fresco by Scotto, also in New York City:

"Service you can teach. Hospitality is in you, and it's a born, bred thing more than it's a situation where you can actually train someone to do it."

the right time after the meal is done. The thing is, how do you motivate the staff to perform these acts?

Many of the actions that can result in a guest's satisfaction are simple enough that almost any employee could be trained to perform them. For instance, getting your maître d' or host to address incoming guests with a smile and a greeting such as "Good evening. How may I help you?" rather than the all-too-common "Do you have a reservation?" is relatively simple, and it starts the customer's dining experience out on a pleasant note. Yet getting your employee to do so with a certain level of warmth and desire to please—which guests will certainly pick up on, just as they will notice its absence—is not quite as simple. You need to make sure the individual greeting guests at the door really enjoys contact with many different kinds of people and shows his or her enthusiasm appropriately. The hiring process for all front of the house employees should include a portion of the interview when the manager can get a sense of the interviewee's personality. Experience is great, but finding a nice person is often more important.

Can hospitality be trained? Sure it can . . . but the employee must have a desire to please the guest for the efforts to ring true.

USING SERVICE TO CREATE HOSPITALITY

BEYOND THE FACT THAT IT HELPS TO HIRE NICE PEOPLE with a desire to please the guests, there are tasks that you can train the staff to perform that will enhance your restaurant's atmosphere of hospitality. The overall type of service depends largely on the kind of establishment you work in; the specific things the staff are asked to do should fit seamlessly into the restaurant's overall demeanor. In the following chart are a number of feelings and reactions that you would want your guests to experience. Listed adjacent to each of those feelings are specific actions that can bring about those feelings.

At the end of the night, when all of the guests and staff members have gone home, you can stand in the middle of your dining room and relive the experiences, good and bad, of that night. One table had the best meal of their lives, while across the room was a person who will never come back because there weren't any meatballs on the menu. There can be euphoria from the series of minor victories that,

A FEW TIPS TO ASSESS A POTENTIAL EMPLOYEE'S PERSONALITY during the interview: take note of the person's handshake, seek out eye contact and see how he or she reacts, and tell a bad joke to see if the person laughs.

taken together, form the mosaic of a perfect night. There can also be the nagging memory of a forgotten birthday candle, the lack of which soured a guest's dinner. Make note of all of these things so that you can share them with the staff before service begins the next day.

All in all, our success and our happiness in this business depend on the delight of our guests, and it's possible to ensure that guests are served in a way that will maximize their pleasure. That is service. That is hospitality.

WELCOMED Offer a smile and a warm, genuine welcome at the front door, such as "Good evening. How may I help you?" Make sure the host's desk faces the door, not the back wall.

PAMPERED Provide valet parking and someone to hold the door open. Make sure guests' coats and umbrellas are taken and stored securely. Have staff pull out chairs for guests as they seat a party.

IMPORTANT Remember and use returning guests' names, and greet them with "Welcome back." Keep track of regular guests' preferences and important dates.

COMFORTABLE Make sure the dining room's heat, lighting levels, and music are appropriate and consistent. Ensure that the dining room is spotlessly clean and that furniture is attractive and in good repair.

ENTERTAINED Offer entertaining tableside preparations or live music, if appropriate. Provide a variety of menu and beverage items, including some novel items unique to your restaurant, and describe them in an enticing way on a menu that is visually interesting.

RELAXED, AT EASE Make sure the reservations process is clear and efficient. Provide waiters with enough knowledge about menu items so that they can answer questions and make suggestions with confidence, and train them in how to read guests' body language so that they can address needs that guests may not feel comfortable expressing. Offer diners choosing wine the expert assistance of a sommelier.

SATIATED Ensure that portion sizes are appropriate (not too big or too small), and instruct waiters to offer guidance if diners seem to be ordering too much or too little food.

APPRECIATED Maintain a "thank you" mailing list. Ask guests for their opinions, and listen carefully to the responses. The key to all the elements in the chart above is that each specific action can be trained. For example, you can train your reservationist to say "May I put you on hold?" and wait for the caller to answer before doing so, so that the potential guest does not feel as if he or she has been dismissed or treated rudely. This is the essence of service—doing things that will lead to a guest's satisfaction.

CHAPTER 2:
THE
RELATIONSHIP
BETWEEN
THE FRONT
AND THE BACK
OF THE HOUSE

When I first started in the restaurant business, I knew that if I was going to be an effective manager, it was critical to know how each component of the restaurant worked. On a prosaic level, if someone gets sick or hurt, the manager has to be able to jump in to complete the job at hand until a more appropriate backup plan can be implemented. On a broader scale, thorough knowledge of each department's needs and capabilities and how they combine to form a whole is vital—it allows the manager to make quick decisions during service so that guests have the positive dining experience they expect.

The kitchen has a tremendous amount of influence on what happens in the dining room. In turn, the kitchen is a production facility, and its success depends on how the front office is managed. For example, if a maître d' books the whole restaurant for a banquet at six o'clock and offers the guests an à la carte menu, all thirty tables' orders get sent in within a few minutes of each other. The kitchen gets slammed and cannot keep up, the guests wait way too long to be served, the dining room staff bears the brunt of the guests' displeasure, and they in turn blame the kitchen personnel, setting up a situation in which everyone loses.

The way to prevent such disasters is to have a thoroughgoing understanding of the roles and responsibilities of those working on the other side of the swinging doors. By knowing how the kitchen works most efficiently, the manager can plan the booking of the dining room in a way that helps the kitchen to serve great food quickly. In the banquet situation described above, an astute manager would offer the guests a set tasting menu that shows off the chef's specialties. The food is sent out in courses, with the cooks traveling from station to station in order to prepare the 120 plates of each course in assembly-line fashion. The guests are served great food in a timely manner, leaving impressed and happy.

The dining room manager has an opportunity to further improve service in the dining room when he or she has a strong knowledge of professional cooking. For example, knowledge of cook times for dishes can make a big difference for the guests. A 36-ounce rib-eye steak for two takes at least forty-five minutes to get to medium rare, while medallions of venison can be cooked to the same doneness in a few minutes. For the guest who is in a hurry, the venison would be the better choice. Waiters should be trained to know how long each dish on the menu takes to cook, and use that information when the guest is ordering. This same knowledge can come in handy when a guest sends back a dish that he or she didn't like, and the waiter needs to offer a replacement. Again, the rib-eye is probably not a good choice—perhaps a pasta or fish dish would be best. One more instance where cook times are important is when guests order main courses without appetizers. If any of the dishes take a long time to cook, the waiter should let the guests know that there will be a bit of a wait for their food.

One other aspect of service that can be eased with the help of the kitchen is setup of the service area. Most trained cooks will put clear soups with small garnishes in bouillon cups, which require the use of a bouillon spoon because large soup spoons won't get to the bottom of the cup. More rustic soups with larger pieces of garnish (vegetables, meat, etc.) go in a soup plate, which gets the larger soup spoon because the bigger garnish won't fit onto a bouillon spoon. Also, if the only pasta on the menu has seafood in it, the waiters won't need to set up bowls of grated cheese, as traditionally there is no cheese served on seafood pastas.

The rest of this chapter will discuss some of the ways that you can develop an understanding of kitchen operations and build a strong, professional working relationship between the kitchen and dining room staffs. This isn't the longest chapter in the book, but it's one of the most important, because a spirit of cooperation between the front of the house and the back is a key ingredient in any restaurant's success.

UNDERSTANDING KITCHEN OPERATIONS

THERE ARE SEVERAL WAYS TO LEARN how a kitchen works. One of the best ways is to attend a culinary school. There is a tremendous variety of schools and programs, each program having its own benefits and demands. It's up to you to decide how much time and money to spend. The major drawback of full-time schooling is the financial commitment and time spent away from your career. Of course, you can look at this expenditure as a lifelong investment in your career. Also, some schools offer shorter courses that can be taken while still working full time.

Another route to learning about the kitchen is by working as an apprentice in a professional kitchen (yours or someone else's). For centuries apprenticeship was the only opportunity to acquire the skills of a particular occupation, and it's still one of the best ways to learn what the restaurant business is really like. An apprenticeship can be even more demanding than cooking school, but the length of it isn't fixed—it's up to you and the person you're apprenticing with. An added benefit of doing an apprenticeship is that the chef you work under may become a mentor and help to guide you throughout your career.

If none of these plans will work, set some time aside to carefully observe the goings-on in a professional kitchen, perhaps the one in the establishment where you work. Watching can be taken one step further by either building some kitchen shifts into your schedule or coming in on your day off to spend a day doing prep work or even cooking on the line. Most chefs and kitchen managers will welcome the free labor and appreciate your desire to learn their side of the business.

Take some time to get to know the chef and what his or her concerns are. Anyone who has been in the food business for more than a few years has probably worked with a difficult chef somewhere along the way, but the fact is that the screamers and knife throwers are far outnumbered by the chefs who are professional and level-headed. Still, chefs and cooks are under a tremendous amount of pressure from the minute they get into the kitchen until the last plate is sent out at the end of the night. What you'll find if you really listen to them is that how the dining room staff operates can make the kitchen staff's jobs easier—or much harder. For instance, if the expediter is constantly overwhelmed by questions from the wait staff, you may need to have the waiters direct all messages to the expediter through the floor manager, who can serve as a sort of filter. You also may find that you're able to help the kitchen by telling them when the last dinner order has been sent in—this will allow the chef to start breaking down stations and cleaning up as soon as possible, which helps save on labor costs.

A strong foundation in all aspects of the dining establishment helps you to make better business decisions, too. Rather than having to wait for the chef to get in before you discuss a menu with some catering clients, for example, you already know what can be done, what will be best for the guest, and, ultimately, what will

UNTIL YOU'VE COOKED PROFESSIONALLY, it's hard to understand the complexity involved in getting four people to cook six different plates of food and have them all ready and perfect at the same time. The rib-eye has to be cooked and must rest before carving, the halibut will take five minutes on the grill, and the fresh pasta literally takes seconds to cook. A thorough understanding of the order-fire-pickup system used by chefs and expediters comes only from being on the inside, in the intense world of the professional kitchen.

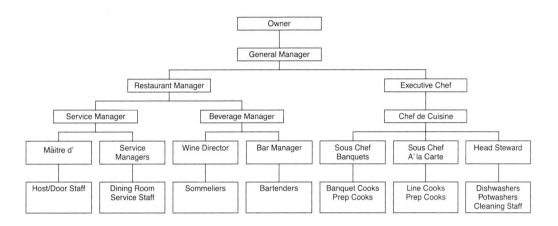

be best for your business. If you can lay out the options to potential clients when they first approach you, you can build on that momentum and perhaps come away with a signed contract after that initial meeting.

If as an owner, you are opening a restaurant without a chef hired yet, it's incredibly important to know how the kitchen will need to be designed and organized and what kitchen equipment will be needed (such as a lobster tank for a seafood shanty). Product knowledge is key as well. Knowing whether fish is fresh or not and how much it should cost can help when the chef isn't around to approve deliveries, and it also helps when keeping an eye on food costs. Certain standard items such as a five-pound box of large shrimp have a price range—you should know what a good (or bad) deal is.

The benefits of learning about the kitchen go beyond the practical information that can help you to make smart decisions with regard to the dining room. One of the greatest of these benefits is the respect that you get from the kitchen staff because of the time and effort you've put into learning about what happens on their side of the wall. What you—and they—will discover is that that the front and back are really on the same side, and can work together to serve the guest.

BUILDING A STRONG RELATIONSHIP WITH THE KITCHEN

THE BASIS OF ANY STRONG RELATIONSHIP is trust and respect. They can be achieved in a number of ways, but both parties have to be in on the deal for it to truly work. For instance, no matter how much a dining room manager professes to know about food, the chef won't respect someone who doesn't know his aspic from his elbow macaroni. The chef and the service manager need to know enough about each other's situations to have mutual respect and understanding. Once this has been established, a trust between the two can be built that will not be shaken by the mistakes and problems that come up on a daily, sometimes hourly, basis.

The benefits of learning what goes on in the chef's domain can also be highly personal. In the course of my own efforts to gain knowledge about the kitchen, I've learned how to cook, and I've learned a bit about wine. But most important, I've been lucky enough to build solid relationships with some great chefs. Working well together led to friendship, which made doing the job together even easier. Do you have to be best friends with your co-workers? Obviously not, but the basic elements of good relationships should be practiced in our workplaces. When the working relationship is at least positive and professional, imbued with respect for each other's abilities, the job is easier to perform. Anger, back-stabbing, and negativity are at least annoying, and in the worst cases they can be damaging enough to derail the whole operation.

I SPOKE RECENTLY TO DENIS FITZGERALD, Executive Chef of Remi in New York. Regarding the relationship between the dining room and the kitchen, he said, "Cooks sometimes don't realize that the waiters have a tough job . . . they just see the waiters asking for food. But I have found that once the kitchen and the dining room realize that they have a common goal—pleasing the guests—the operation starts to run better."

I KNOW A DINING ROOM MANAGER who worked in a restaurant with an unreasonable executive chef. The chef worked very short hours, and when he was in the restaurant he was abusive toward the entire dining room staff. As the relationship between chef and manager became more strained, communication between front and back became virtually nonexistent. Guests suffered, the staff was unhappy, and the atmosphere of the restaurant took on a negative aspect. Eventually, the manager left this unhappy situation by finding a new job. The chef eventually was fired. The same restaurant now has a chef who communicates effectively with the rest of the management team and who is well liked by the floor and kitchen staffs. From what I've heard, everybody is happier at work now, and the guests are benefiting from the improved relationships.

Establishing mutual respect might not be as hard as you think. One of the easiest ways to get started on it is to be effective in your position. If there is one thing that a professional appreciates in someone, it's a job well done. This isn't to say that you have to spend twenty hours a day at work—in fact, that can hurt your reputation. It's not the amount of time spent at work but how effective you are in your job that can gain you instant respect from your counterparts in the kitchen.

Another respect builder is being able to admit fault and to confess ignorance. Neither of these is an easily acquired habit, but both are worth cultivating. Human nature leads us to conceal our mistakes and to avoid honesty if it means showing weakness. Rather than hiding the sheet pan of burned bacon, or blaming the busser for the guest's empty water glass, owning up to the error helps in several ways. First of all, it locates the problem and can lead more quickly to a proper solution. Second, it helps to build trust between the staff, and it earns respect for the person who was strong enough to admit error. Realistically, the person who repeatedly makes the same mistakes probably doesn't belong on the staff, but the honest mistakes that we all make occasionally should be allowed and treated with understanding, because we learn from our mistakes.

INCLUDING THE CHEF IN
DINING ROOM OPERATIONS

YOUR CHEF IS A MANAGER, too. Just as co-managers in other businesses often consult each other when making decisions, you would be well served by considering the professional opinions of your kitchen counterpart. The manager and chef should meet on a regular basis to discuss the menu, service issues, the beverage program, reservations, and any other matters of concern.

The chef is very conscious of what the kitchen is capable of producing, and at what rate. If you're thinking about changing your reservations system, for example, the chef should be involved in the planning process, because he or she will be in the best position to know the number of covers per hour the kitchen is capable of turning out. Or let's say a theater opens next door, and so the possibility of a pre-theater menu pops up. The chef could certainly come up with the menu on his or her own, but by working together the two of you will probably come up with a more workable and more creative solution.

It's not just the chef who should be included in these discussions, either. Service improves significantly when the waiters know more about the food, and pre-service meetings are more useful when the food information being disseminated by the manager comes directly from the chef. Even better, the chef can attend these meetings and discuss the food directly with the waiters. In turn, servers can provide helpful information to the chef about what the guests like and dislike about the existing menu, and what sorts of dishes they inquire about that aren't presently on the menu. For instance, at Campagna in New York, the waiters were getting more and more requests for chopped salads at lunch. Without hesitation, Mark Strausman, the chef and owner, added the Madison Salad to the menu. This delicious mix of chopped tuna, beets, lentils, shallots, mesclun, and a host of other ingredients quickly became one of the best-selling items on the lunch menu.

You should also consider having your chef pay occasional visits to the dining room when feasible. The celebrity chef has become a part of our dining culture, and the presence of your own "celebrity" in the dining room, in sparkling kitchen whites and toque, can engage guests in a way that no maître d' ever could. This is not just an image booster, either—there can be the extra benefit of giving the chef a chance to interact with customers and get some direct feedback on the menu and the food.

WHY CAN'T WE ALL GET ALONG?

OUR BUSINESS IS HARD ENOUGH without the bickering and difficulties brought on by a flawed relationship between the front and the back of the house. Rivalry between the two is rarely anything but harmful to the staff and, ultimately, the business. Cooks calling waiters "coffee slappers" and waiters referring to cooks as "range rovers" is occasionally good for a laugh, but it's not the way to build a solid team.

Chefs in dining rooms, dining room managers in kitchens—from that initial step can come benefits that reach every single member of the staff. Not only does a productive relationship between chef and manager make it easier to do your jobs, but employees benefit from the more efficiently run workplace and are given a good model to follow. Cooperation starts at the top and spreads throughout the workplace.

The more we all know about the whole, the easier it becomes to serve our guests. The job itself is more manageable because decisions can be made more quickly and accurately. It's also more enjoyable—positive relationships with co-workers make the atmosphere more pleasant, and we can work from a more solid emotional base. The restaurant business is a jungle; we really do need each other to survive.

CHAPTER 3:
THE FRONT DOOR

T That old saw about first impressions is true—they're important, and you only have one chance. The initial contact that potential guests have with your place of business must be welcoming and overwhelmingly positive, and it starts even before they've arrived at your doorstep.

THE VIRTUAL FRONT DOOR

THE INTERNET IS NOW A PART OF OUR RESTAURANT WORLD, like it or not. People who are looking for a place to eat are as likely to surf the Net to find a restaurant as they are to read a guidebook or look in the Yellow Pages. You must have a presence on the Internet, even if it's only your address and phone number. If you want to have some control of your virtual image, perhaps it's time to carve out a corner for yourself on the Web. There are several ways for you to do this, with different levels of involvement and financial outlay.

Perhaps the easiest is to work with on-line restaurant directories that, for a nominal fee, will list information about your restaurant on a page with similar information about other local restaurants. Almost every city has at least one or two such firms. To find them, just pick a search engine and look for some local restaurants. Chances are some of the smaller restaurants will be listed on one of these group sites. When signing up for this service, you can go for just the basics, such as address, phone number, and hours of operation. As you add information, such as menus and wine lists, more pages are required, which will add to your fee. Also, menus and such need to be updated regularly, which will require more time and attention from you. Using a service like this is a relatively easy way to gain a presence on the Web but lacks personality. Indeed, you don't have *any* creative control over your Web site, but the job gets done with a minimum of muss and fuss.

Another option is to hire a Web designer to do your site for you. The sky is the limit as to how much time and money you spend on this process. Web site design charges can vary wildly, from the affordable recent design school graduate to the top-dollar big-name firm. The benefits of using this approach are many—clean page design, efficient site navigation, and the possibility of regular updates by a computer professional. The biggest downside is cost. The more you want to do, the more expensive it gets. One other, less cumbersome shortcoming is the lack of personal input. Some Web designers have a formula or style that might not fit in with your vision.

The third way of doing this, for some people, is the best way: do it yourself. There are many Web site design programs available now that are relatively easy to learn and fairly straightforward to use, especially if you are proficient with a PC. The days of having to write everything in HTML code are over, and the do-it-yourselfer has several affordable options. The programs themselves are not terribly expensive, so the greatest investment you make will be your time. Paying someone with a server to host your site is also quite affordable. Once again, how much time you can invest in the process will be the determining factor in the final quality of your website.

One of these three approaches will fit your needs, a big part of which is budget. The most important thing is that you have a virtual front door for guests to knock on . . . and walk through.

RESERVATIONS SYSTEMS

RECENTLY A RESTAURANT OPENED in my town, and the owners decided to take reservations only for parties of six or more. There was a lot of hype already built up, and many area residents had high expectations for this new place, so business was brisk at the outset. Yet some members of the community were put off by the system. They wanted to be able to make reservations for a Friday or Saturday night for fewer than six. Having been made aware of this grumbling, the owners had a choice to make: stick to their guns and keep people waiting for their tables, or take reservations for any size party. They did the former. The place has never been busier, but there is a cadre of locals who will never set foot in the restaurant.

Another nearby restaurant, the Chart House, ran for years with a wait list and no reservations. For years customers would put their name in, then wait up to two hours for a table on the busiest nights. As competing restaurants in the area began opening, customers didn't feel the need to wait for a table at the Chart House, and business there went down. With the introduction of a reservations system, though, the "Charties" were right back in the game—they're now reporting the same sales as they were before the competition arrived.

The question of whether or not to accept reservations is not a simple one to answer, but it's likely one you'll have to deal with sooner or later. I've worked in hugely successful restaurants that operated on a first-come, first-served basis and had lines out the door. I have also worked in places where you almost had to interview with the owner to get a reservation. The factors that you have to consider when making this decision are as follows:

- **STYLE OF RESTAURANT.** Is the style of your place formal or casual? The fancier the restaurant, the more likely it is that you will need to accept reservations. A couple planning their anniversary dinner will often choose a more formal restaurant, and they almost certainly won't be interested in waiting an hour for their table to open up. Conversely, when you and your friends are going out for Mexican food as a group, it's usually fine if you wind up waiting in the bar of the cantina, drinking margaritas and eating chips and salsa.

- **NUMBER OF SEATS.** The number of seats in the dining room is usually decided early in the planning stages of a restaurant and is integral to the type of service. A casual restaurant tends to have more seats with tables closer together; the opposite is true for more formal restaurants. A large casual restaurant tends to turn tables faster, and usually has a table coming available soon; thus, reservations might not be necessary. However, in a formal restaurant where people usually take more time to eat and the number of seats is limited, tables don't free up as quickly—this might be the right place to take reservations.

- **PROJECTED NUMBER OF COVERS PER NIGHT.** Like the number of seats, the amount of covers you're planning on doing is rather important. A high volume of tables that turn over quickly might not require a reservation policy.

- **HOW POPULAR IS YOUR RESTAURANT?** The more famous or visible a restaurant or restaurateur, the higher the demand for tables. For instance, if Emeril opens a restaurant in your neighborhood, you would definitely check out the reservations policy before getting your hopes up. Meanwhile, a chef with no reputation might open on a first-come, first-served basis, then start offering reservations as the place gets more popular and finds it necessary to spread the diners across the period of service rather than taking them whenever they want to come in.

- **OTHER FACTORS.** If you're next door to a theater, there might be an entire seating of the restaurant that leaves before eight o'clock, and one that comes after the show. Done right, you can have the pre-theater, dinner, and post-theater crowds arranged into three seatings. Being near a convention center can make a difference also, so you should know when a show or group is coming into town and be ready, perhaps, for more business than usual.

Although intuition is a powerful and often accurate way of deciding which way to go, the answer is always in the sales numbers. As you experiment with different reservations policies, keep them in place long enough to get a good sample of sales figures for each one. Weekly, monthly, and annual sales figures are a very good barometer of success (or failure) and should have some influence on your final decision.

NO RESERVATIONS

If you have decided to go with a first-come, first-served system, you'll find that it's relatively easy to work with . . . until the room fills up. Now you have to figure out how to implement a waiting list.

Have you ever wondered how hosts are able to look at a list of names and confidently tell you that it would be twenty minutes for a table? To tell you the truth, they may wonder how they do it, too—it's a skill that comes largely with experience. The more experience the host has in your restaurant, the more accurate his or her estimates will be.

The estimate is based on many factors: average guest stay, number of large parties, how fast the kitchen is sending out plates, and even the unquantifiable factor of how the place simply *feels* that night. The best hosts will take all of the available criteria, analyze them, come up with an accurate estimate, and then add five minutes to play it safe. The more accurate the estimates are, the more business you will do; people who decide to wait and are able to sit down on time will be happy with the result and will probably return. The ones who decide not to wait might well come back someday to see what the hubbub is about, and they might stay that next time.

If, however, the host consistently underestimates wait times, it will eventually hurt your business. Guests who have to wait an hour instead of twenty minutes will be very upset once they get to the table, and the waiter will be expected to tap-dance and juggle to make them happy. Even worse is when people walk out because the wait was longer than they expected—good luck getting *them* to come back.

Needless to say, if you are going with a no-reservations system, you are hoping that there will soon be the need for a waiting list. Just make sure that the people at

ADVANTAGES OF A NO-RESERVATIONS POLICY	DISADVANTAGES OF A NO-RESERVATIONS POLICY
Reduces personnel needed to staff the phones	Crowds can scare away potential customers—that is, the Yogi Berra syndrome can kick in: "Nobody goes there anymore, it's too crowded"
Maximizes table use through constant turnover	The service staff may feel compelled to rush diners to free up tables
Eliminates the no-show problem and lends a more casual aura to an establishment	Customers may get tired of waiting and leave or tell their friends not to bother; also, some customers will not patronize a restaurant if they are not guaranteed a table
Increases bar sales—even if guests waiting for tables do not buy a drink, a busy bar creates a lively ambience and attracts more bar business	The decibel level can mount as guests waiting at the bar sip their drinks
People standing outside give passers by the impression that this is an "in" place	Additional space is needed for people to wait, especially in cold weather

ADVANTAGES OF A ACCEPTING RESERVATIONS	DISADVANTAGES OF ACCEPTING RESERVATIONS
Makes some guests feel more comfortable to have a guaranteed table	Requires extra staff to work the reservation desk and make confirmation calls
Helps a restaurant estimate customer flow, which is better for kitchen and dining room staffs as well as guests	Creates a no-show problem, which skews sales projections and estimates
Allows more efficient table assignments	Requires extra effort on the part of customers who might otherwise just drop in at the last minute
Allows a restaurant to become familiar with customers' names and eating preferences	
Makes it easier to deal with special requests (birthdays, special menus, allergies, etc.), since they can be handled at the time of reservation rather than after the customer arrives	
Permits logging the phone numbers of guests for future promotions or in case they leave something behind	
Some restaurants use both reservation methods—reservations may be required only for large groups, for example	

your door have the support and training to do the job well, and let them know how important they are to the success of the restaurant. The hosts are making money for you.

With such a system, the operative word is, of course, *system*. Maintain the waitlist on a legal pad, sure, but next to the guest's name, write the current time and the quoted wait time. When the table is ready for the guest, some hosts will walk through the bar calling the guest's name while other restaurants, like the Hilltop Steakhouse in Saugus, MA, have a public address system. It's going to be a long time before I forget hearing "Fischer party to Carson City! Fischer party to the Carson City Room!" Still other restaurants have electronic pagers that they will hand to the guest once their name has been logged. When the table is ready, the host pushes a button and somewhere, a pager starts vibrating. It's not a foolproof system, because guests sometimes misplace the pagers, but it can cut down on the number of annoying announcements.

TAKING RESERVATIONS

RESERVATIONS SYSTEMS

If you've decided to establish a reservations system for your new place, your next decision involves choosing the system that works best for you. There are hundreds if not thousands of ways to take reservations, from yellow Post-it Notes and cocktail napkins to highly complex computer programs. Most are somewhere in the middle, involving the use of a reservations book.

Restaurant Reservations

	#	Name	Table	Comments
11:30	4	Gurian, Judith		
	2	Dodd, Peter		
	2	Farrell, Mary		
	2	McCarthy, Vincent		
	2	McGee, Lisa		
	4	Tan, Carmilla		
	16			
12:00	13	Shandoff, Jane	32,33	Dep. $160
	4	Noah, Dr. Harold		Rose room w/window
	3	Draper, James		Booked through Carol Dipper
	3	Davis, Kerry		
	23			
12:30	2	Royalty, Linda		
	6	Purello, Eugene		
	3	Brandon, Patricia		
	5	Momjian, Joan		
	4	Ensley, Rhonda		2 b-days, 4 adults and 8 wk baby
	5	Ferringo, Joseph		4 adults, one 8 year old
	25			
1:00	2	Kramer, Douglas		
	2	Kelly, Richmond		
	4	Goldberg, William		
	2	Ashley, Suzanne		
	10			
Total	74			

I do not personally recommend the Post-it Note and cocktail napkin method, which invariably leads to the six-top that shows up on New Year's Eve at ten o'clock and says they made a reservation months before. A classic reservations book, or even copies of reservation sheets, will get you started.

One step up from the pencil-and-paper method is to input the information into a spreadsheet program. You could also link a spreadsheet to your database in order to keep track of regular customers' birthdays, anniversaries, likes, dislikes, and dietary restrictions. The more information you have at your fingertips, the higher the level of hospitality that you can provide for your guests.

There are also computer programs that are specifically designed to accept and keep track of restaurant and hotel reservations. Some of them can be maintained by your own staff. In addition, there are Web-based companies that can manage your reservations while maintaining a database of your guests' pertinent information, such as mailing addresses, birthdays, allergies, personal preferences, and so on. The downside of such systems is lack of complete control and privacy.

INFORMATION NEEDED TO MAKE A RESERVATION

Whichever system you choose, the bare bones of information you need to have for a reservation are as follows:

- **GUEST'S NAME.** Both first name and last name are important, since some last names are common, and you might take reservations from two or more people with the same name for the same night.

- **DATE THE RESERVATION IS FOR.**

- **TIME THE RESERVATION IS FOR.**

- **NUMBER OF PEOPLE IN THE PARTY.**

- **DATE THAT THE RESERVATION WAS TAKEN.** This bit of information may seem less obvious than the four previously listed, but it can be useful when you have to decide which of two reservations should get the window table that both requested. The guests who called first should get it.

- **GUEST'S DAY AND EVENING PHONE NUMBERS FOR CONFIRMATION.** Phone numbers are very important. The confirmation process not only helps to you plan ahead but lets the guest know that you are on top of things. It also gives you a chance to gently but firmly request that guests notify you if there are any changes in their plans.

- **A NOTE OF SPECIAL REQUESTS SUCH AS BIRTHDAYS, ANNIVERSARIES, OR A SPECIAL TABLE.** Some sort of space for comments should always be included in your reservations system. In addition to noting special requests, you can also use this space for information about the guest's likes and dislikes. If you know that one of your regulars doesn't like specific items, this is one place to put that information, as you might not be there to make sure the guest gets his spaghetti without basil in the tomato sauce.

- **NAME OR INITIALS OF THE PERSON TAKING THE RESERVATION.** This is important when you need more clarification about a reservation, such as whose birthday it is. The person who took the information may remember that detail, sparing you the need to call the guest.

Many restaurants now ask for a credit card number to hold the reservation. The implication, of course, is that there will be some sort of penalty if the guest doesn't show up. Unless agreed to by the guest though, it is illegal to do so. In my experience, doing this makes the guest uncomfortable and can put him or her into a bad humor. I prefer not to scare guests into coming to dinner. However, in the case of a large party (twenty or more guests), it is smart to get either a signed contract with penalties for late cancellations, or just take a deposit that is not refundable within certain proximity to the date of the reservation.

One other thing: if you're using a paper-based system, write in pencil. Things happen.

OVERBOOKING

The practice of taking more reservations than you have capacity for is rather common in the restaurant business. One reason this is done is to make up for the

TO CONFIRM RESERVATIONS, a member of the reservations staff will call the guest a day or two before the reservation date to make sure they're still coming. You might be surprised by the number of people who have changed their plans, but not called the restaurant. Some restaurants even ask the customer to call and confirm. I think it's more hospitable for the restaurant to do the calling.

PHONE ETIQUETTE

THE PERSON WHO ANSWERS the phone is a representative of your establishment and is often the first contact that a guest will have. Therefore, this person must have good phone skills. First things first: always answer the phone within three rings. A good way to start is with a clear, friendly greeting, such as "Good morning, Bubba's Place, may I help you?" Always say "Good morning" if it's before noon, "Good afternoon" between noon and five o'clock, and "Good evening" thereafter. You can also add your name, as in "Good afternoon, Southwestern Grill, Patty speaking, may I help you?" but whether or not to give one's name when answering the phone is more of a style issue than manners.

Here are some other tips:

- Before putting someone on hold, say "May I put you on hold?"—and then wait for the guest to answer before you actually push the hold button. The guest may not be able to wait, and he or she may simply want a quick piece of information.

- When picking up a line on hold, say "Thank you for holding, how may I help you?"

- Repeat information back to the guest when you're taking a reservation: "So, that's five people for dinner at seven-thirty on Friday, December 5, for Marian Evans; is that correct?" And whenever a credit card number is involved, the entire number should be confirmed, including expiration date.

- Write down everything; never trust short-term memory.

- Have information at hand that will help the phone people answer the questions they'll be asked most often. You can create a fact sheet that covers directions, menu information, dress code, history of the restaurant, even bios of the chef and owner. There should also be a folder with current menus that can be faxed to a guest who calls and asks for one. (It must be someone's job to keep these menus updated so that guests won't be sent the Asparagus Festival menu in February.)

inevitable no-shows who do not honor their reservation and do not call to cancel. Overbooking to hedge against lost sales because of no-shows can be done in a sensible manner. The trick is to keep good reservation records and figure out the average percentage of guests who do not show up for dinner and don't call beforehand to cancel. Even more precisely, you might want to see if the percentages change depending on the day of the week—for instance, many restaurants experience higher no-show percentages on Saturday nights. Once average percentages have been calculated, you can overbook by that number. There is a chance, of course, that everybody will show up, and then the challenge is to keep the waiting time low and the guests happy.

Some establishments overbook just to keep the place packed all the time. This can be dangerous, because while a few minutes' wait here or there is understandable to most guests, forcing guests to wait long past their reservation time on a consistent basis will make them angry, which is definitely not good business. It also isn't fair: if the restaurant expects guests to show up on time for their reservations, the table should be ready when they get there.

TOO SLOW	TOO BUSY
Waiters chitchatting	Guests aren't being greeted properly
Host falling asleep	Printer in kitchen resembles tickertape machine
Coat checker doing crossword puzzle	Waiters don't know their own names
Cooks playing liar's poker	Guests checking milk cartons for picture of their waiter
Bartender working on new pickle martini	Bartender forgets recipe for scotch and soda

HOW MANY TO TAKE?

Now that you've decided to accept reservations, you have to figure out how many people to take and when. You have just so many tables and chairs. How they get filled will determine the level of service you will be able to provide, and how much business you will do.

Although it may sound somewhat counterintuitive, you should not fill the place up the minute the doors are opened. Let's take a look at one possible scenario. It's six o'clock, and guests with reservations are lined up outside. The host opens the door, and the dining room is instantly full. Waiters run from table to table—greet, greet, greet; drinks, drinks, drinks; order, order, order. The bartender is in the weeds, and all of the dinner orders hit the kitchen at the same time. The sauté station has twelve veal scaloppini on order and shares six burners with the poissonier, who also has a full slate of orders. So although you may look proudly at the full dining room, service will be far from perfect because the entire *staff* is in the weeds—drinks take too long, bread never shows up, the waiters are rushed, and the kitchen is physically incapable of sending out all of the food that was ordered in that fifteen-minute period. Some food will come out earlier than guests want, some later, making the diners unhappy. And there's a downside financially as well—those guests who get their food late will therefore be leaving later, and longer stay times result in fewer table turns, which in turn means lower sales.

Think of the restaurant as a machine. If you feed it a certain number of guests every fifteen minutes (instead of all at once), the waiters have time to get each table started, the bartender is working at a steady, if busy, rate, and the dinner orders are going into the kitchen in a nice, steady flow. The restaurant machine works more efficiently. Instead of huge peaks of activity and valleys of inactivity, a steady (but intense) influx of business allows everyone in the restaurant to perform at peak level.

Every restaurant is unique, and peak efficiency is achieved at different rates of customer influx. There's no secret formula because it depends on style of service, the menu, and even the clientele. Here, though, are some indicators for you:

All kidding aside, you will have to determine the number of covers per hour (or half-hour, or quarter-hour) that will optimize service in your restaurant. A good way to determine that number is to start conservatively. As noted in Chapter 2, the chef, who knows the capabilities of the kitchen better than anyone else in the restaurant, can give you valuable input here. Once you've settled on a number, over the course of a few days increase covers per hour until you see the machine bogging down, then back off a touch.

Restaurants often have a range of table sizes, some for two, four—even eight and ten. When planning the reservations for an evening, the reservationist takes into account that larger tables almost always take longer to dine than smaller groups. So, a certain table for eight might only be booked for two seatings while deuces right next to that big table will be turned four or five times.

Large parties, especially those taking up an entire room in the restaurant, will often be it for the night. It depends, of course, on the speed of service, but there is often table-hopping and socializing that doesn't happen when there's just one table for the party. Take advantage of this, though, and suggest a cocktail hour with hors d'oeuvres and perhaps some live music. Since you won't be turning the tables, sell them more stuff to compensate.

Menu and staffing changes (including training) can increase your efficiency, so remain flexible. Also, if you make major changes to the style of your restaurant (such as adding tablecloths and candles), watch for signs of service slowing down. It's not necessarily a bad thing, though, because you can raise prices a little to counter the loss of revenue from reduced covers.

WALK-INS

Every restaurant will have guests coming through the front door without reservations. If there's a free table, of course they should be seated and served. If there isn't any unreserved space, they can be offered a seat at the bar to wait for a cancellation or no-show . . . with the caveat that this might not happen.

When that walk-in is a regular customer, it's a good idea to get them a table as soon as possible. At Campagna, we had a reservation policy, but we also had a lot of regulars who had specific tables that were "theirs." We would get calls from them often, saying that they were "on their way over" and wanted their table. Usually, if it was already taken we would offer another table nearby and they understood because of the late notice. Sometimes, if the table was simply unavailable, we ended up with an unhappy executive standing in the middle of the dining room. For some of these people, we would actually keep "their" table open when we knew that this person was in town that week. This extra work on our part created an extremely loyal clientele. Was it worth it? We figured out that about two-thirds of our business came from one-third of our clientele. It was worth it.

HOW TO RUN THE DOOR

THE DOOR IS NOT JUST AN entrance, it's a concept. There are both physical and psychological aspects to the door, and all of them should be attended to.

PHYSICAL PRESENTATION

First of all, the front of your restaurant should be well maintained and clean. Whether consciously or subliminally, the guest will have a reaction to the condition of your entrance. Make sure you attend to the following:

- Hardware (such as door handles) should be working properly and shined so that it gleams.

- Glass on the door should be sparkling clean.

- Any trash on the sidewalk should be removed.

- Put down floor mats when it's raining or snowy, and keep them clean.

- Keep ashtrays clean (I especially like the ones with a logo imprinted in the sand).

A grungy entrance can cause the guest to wonder about the cleanliness of the entire facility. At the very least, it's not a good way to start off someone's meal at your place. Make a staff member responsible for the condition of the door during service.

GREETING GUESTS

When guests walk in the door, there *must* be someone there to greet them. One person has to be responsible for the door. I hate it when I walk into a restaurant that's bustling with activity, but there's nobody at the front desk—it makes me wonder if I should be there at all. Uncertainty is not a good first feeling to give your guests.

Keep in mind that responsibility for the door does not mean shackling some poor staffer to the front desk. It means that one person is in charge of making sure that the door (and phone, if the restaurant doesn't have a separate phone room) is covered. If you split the responsibility among several people, you'll soon hear "Well, *he* said it was covered."

Here are a few tips to make a great first impression on guests:

- **ARRANGE THE FRONT DESK SO THAT IT FACES THE DOOR.** This alerts guests where to go when they walk in.

- **NEVER LET A HOST, GREETER, OR MAÎTRE D' STAND WITH HIS OR HER BACK TO THE DOOR.** Walking into a restaurant and seeing someone's back does not give the guest a warm feeling of welcome—instead, it feels forbidding.

- **GREET GUESTS IMMEDIATELY, AND MAKE EYE CONTACT.** There's nothing worse than a guest standing awkwardly in the entry while staffers chat among themselves or stare at the reservation book.

- **GREET THE GUEST WITH "GOOD EVENING, HOW MAY I HELP YOU?"** Don't forget to change the greeting depending on the time of day. And never, ever have your first words to the guests be "Do you have a reservation?"

- **USE GUESTS' NAMES WHENEVER POSSIBLE.** This is especially valuable with repeat customers—it sets a wonderful tone.

- **DON'T ASSUME THAT EVERYONE STANDING BEFORE THE DESK BELONGS TO THE SAME PARTY.** If four people arrive at the same time, they may be two separate parties, or even part of a larger group. Ask how many are in the party.

- **OFFER TO TAKE COATS AND BAGS.** This can be a relief for guests, especially if it's rainy outside or they're loaded down with packages, and it makes them feel cosseted. Fancier restaurants tend to have a coat check area or dedicated room to store guests' belongings while they are dining. There should, of course, be coat racks with numbered hangers, shelves for hats and personal items, and even a bucket or stand to store dripping umbrellas.

- **CONFIRM RESERVATION INFORMATION, IF NEED BE.**

The staffers working the door should never go away from the desk to perform service duties, leaving the door unattended. You may need to have more than one person working the door to make sure that this doesn't happen.

If you are working the door and not actively greeting guests, keep an eye on the dining room and be alert to any possible trouble spots. If you see any, inform the manager.

SEATING

ONCE YOU'VE GREETED THE GUESTS and made them feel welcome, it's time to decide where to seat them. Seating the dining room sets everything else in motion, and the way in which it is done will determine your level of success on two levels. First, the number of guests you will be able to accommodate depends on how quickly people can be served and how fast tables can be turned. When the room is seated properly, efficiency is maximized—the floor and the kitchen are both working at a peak level. Second, proper seating means that the service itself will be better. When guests are seated at the correct intervals, waiters have time to be attentive to the guests' needs, rather than rushing around.

What this all points to is that your host or maître d' is an incredibly important part of the staff, with a tremendous amount of influence on your bottom line. Hire and train with this in mind, and keep the good ones as long as possible! All practical reasons aside, your regular guests get to know and appreciate a familiar face at the door. When the relationship between staff and customer acquires a patina of emotional warmth, that's when true hospitality is being provided, and when we are at our best.

WHERE SHOULD THEY SIT?

Some call it an art, others a science; still others think there's more than a little voodoo involved. Whatever you want to call it, the intelligent seating of a dining room is the final piece in the puzzle of how to bring people in, and one of the most important with regard to the quality of service you will provide and, consequently, how much money will be made in the process.

There are as many ways of seating a dining room as there are maître d's. There are several key factors in the process of intelligent seating, and to be able to make intelligent decisions about who is going to sit where, all of them must be attended to.

- **DON'T SLAM WAITERS WITH MORE THAN ONE OR TWO TABLES AT A TIME.** The host or maître d' should rotate arriving parties through the stations, giving the waiters a couple of minutes to get each table started. Even in an incredibly busy restaurant this can be done, because ten minutes gives the waiter time to greet, get a drink order, and maybe even submit the dinner order before the next table shows up. This also helps avoid logjams in the kitchen caused by a whole slew of orders coming in at once, and so it contributes to raising the overall level of service in the restaurant.

TAKING COATS AND BAGS, while hospitable, can hold a lot of responsibility for the restaurateur. Laptops, fur coats, important papers in briefcases, and even the lowly raincoat can all be of tremendous value to the guest, and a liability for the restaurant. It might be smart to post a sign at the coat check stand stating that the staff cannot be held responsible for lost or damaged items. To be certain, talk to a lawyer and insurance agent to make sure you are covered.

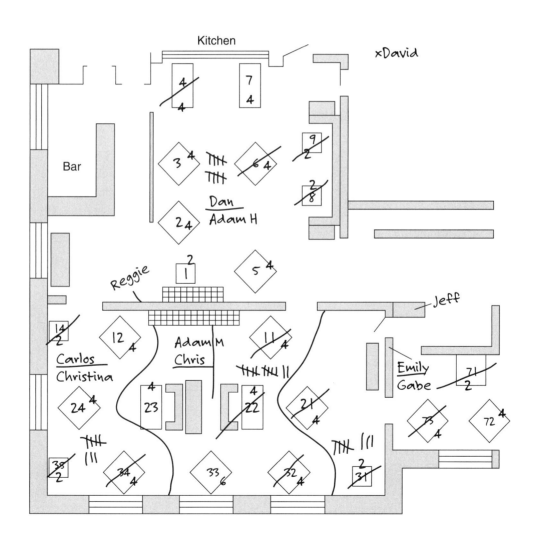

There are several good reasons to divide the business equally between the waiters. First of all, it evens out the workload so there won't be one station with twenty-three guests and another with seven. Even though less busy waiters can help those with more guests, there is a big difference between a waiter's desire to please his or her own customers and the need to help someone else's. Another reason is so that the waiters will all have the same potential for tips. The amounts of the tips might not be controllable, but the manager has done due diligence by giving each station an equal (or comparable) number of covers. I have found that a good way to manage this is to keep a running total of covers in each station. I do this with hash marks on a paper copy of the floor plan that has the sections delineated. This enables me to see at a glance how many covers are in a station, and who needs to get sat next.

- **TRY TO SEAT THE BEST TABLES IN THE HOUSE FIRST, GRADUALLY MOVING TO THE WORST.** Best can mean best view, quietest, or most visible, and worst can mean worst view, nearest the kitchen, or in the back where no one can see you—it all depends on the restaurant. For example, in waterside restaurants, the window tables should go first, then the next row in, and so on. When dividing up the sections, try to divvy up the best tables to avoid the slam.

  If several good tables are available, try to offer the guests a choice: "Would you like to sit where you can watch the chef in our open kitchen, or would you prefer to be by the window?" While many cities and towns have adopted no-smoking policies for restaurants, others still allow smoking indoors. In these locales, it's important to determine smoking preference when the reservation is taken. Sometimes, of course, there is only one table that will work, in which case the host brings the guests to that table and says a little prayer.

- **KEEP TRACK OF THE TIME EACH TABLE WAS SEATED.** Keep a clock at the host stand and write the time next to the name on the reservation sheet or the floor plan. This way you'll know which section got the most recent party of guests, and which should be next.

CHAPTER 4:
PREPARATION FOR
SERVICE

It has been said that preparation is everything. It's as true in the hospitality industry as it is anywhere else. In our business, it can refer to the big picture, such as staff training that leads to optimal performance. It can also be seen in little details, such as prefolded wine service napkins on the bar.

With a few hundred customers, both regulars and newbies, coming in for dinner, there is a lot of work to do. Just as in preparing your home to welcome dinner-party guests you clean, shop, set the table, buy flowers, and set up a bar, a very similar series of tasks needs to be carried out in order to prepare the restaurant for service.

WHO DOES WHAT?

IT STANDS TO REASON that staffers generally handle the setup of the areas that they have primary responsibility for. The bartender sets up the bar. Waiters work on their tables and the items that they will be using during service, such as flatware and linens. Bussers cut bread, fill water pitchers, and fold napkins. The host or hostess wipes down menus, replaces the ones in the worst condition with new ones, and looks over the reservation book.

None of this is written in stone, of course, but tasks should usually be assigned to those who will have to live with the results. On the other hand, unconventional assignments—such as waiters setting up the bar, the bartender folding napkins or polishing silver—could help to even out the workload in the restaurant, and it can give some employees a better understanding of how the whole operation works and help encourage a spirit of teamwork.

The first thing to do is to make a list of every task that needs to be completed in order to open the restaurant for business. What gets included on this list will depend on many factors. For instance, the outdoor café won't have to be set up in January if the restaurant is in Maine, unless the local Polar Bear Club has a reservation. Every detail of the dining room and dining experience should be considered fodder for the list. Every need of the guest should be considered, including items such as black napkins to avoid white lint on dark outfits, simple syrup to sweeten iced tea (instead of granulated sugar, which can take a long time to dissolve in a chilled drink), and reading glasses for guests who forget their own.

Menu changes, the addition of tableside preparations, and changes to the interior of the restaurant can create new needs for the setup list, so the list of tasks to be carried out should be under constant scrutiny. Also, it will become apparent that

there are some inequities—some staff members will have too much work, while some will be standing around drinking coffee. Give the coffee drinkers something to do and lighten up on the overburdened folks.

Keep in mind also that some setup jobs are more onerous than others, and you should try to spread them around fairly. Silver polishing is not everyone's idea of merrymaking, so it can be split up among a few people, or even assigned on a rotating basis.

SERVICE CHECKLISTS

Many restaurants use opening and closing checklists. The items most often included on such lists are covered below.

WAITERS' RESPONSIBILITIES

- Chairs
- China
- Coffee equipment
- Condiments
- Creamers
- Floral and wine displays
- Flatware and holloware
- Floor
- Garbage containers
- Glasses
- Gueridons or side tables
- Linen
- Pantry
- Pitchers
- Reach-in refrigerator
- Side stands
- Soup cart
- Tables
- Trays
- Tray stands
- Trolleys (voitures)

MAÎTRE D'

- Check reservation book
- Discuss cover count and flow with chef
- Communicate any special requests to the chef and staff
- Explain seating requirements to the floor staff
- Adjust temperature, lighting, and music

SERVICE STAFF: HOSTS, WAITERS, AND BUSSERS

- Arrange tables and chairs according to reservations
- Maintain proper space between tables
- Repair wobbly tables
- Wipe tables and counters clean
- Lay tablecloths or set placemats
- Fold napkins for tables, resetting, and serviettes
- Polish any serviceware, hollowware, flatware, china, and glasses
- Fill and wipe condiment containers, salt and pepper shakers, etc.
- Set the tables
- Fill wine buckets halfway with ice and water (just prior to service)
- Prep any underliners on plates or bar trays
- Prep decrumbing plates, placing napkin and crumber with appropriate plate
- Prepare silver transport plates
- Stock dupe pads or order-taking forms
- Stock check printer area
- Check supply of staples (for stapling credit card vouchers and so on)

CLOSING DUTIES FOR SERVICE STAFF

- Return all foodstuffs to the kitchen
- Clear tables
- Stack chairs
- Clean, refill, and refrigerate condiment containers as necessary
- Replenish china, glassware, and flatware
- Clean shelves and trays
- Clean pantry and reach-in
- Adjust lighting and dining room temperature

MANAGING SETUP

THE MANAGER CAN'T DO ALL OF THE SETUP chores but does have to make sure that they're getting done. A hierarchy must be established that will ensure an efficient setup before every service. A classic business chain of command will work here. The owner should be able to walk into the place at any time and not have to worry if there are enough folded napkins. That is because the general manager gives his or her managers the responsibility of monitoring the work in progress and getting the restaurant open on time and in perfect shape. The managers on duty (sometimes called MODs) have the checklists, and often the responsibility of writing and modifying them to keep up with necessary changes. There can be one more layer of management, where a headwaiter or captain will oversee the waiters and bussers as they progress in their duties. Maintain this structure and you won't have an assistant manager folding napkins in the back when he or she should be on the floor watching the waiters.

SETTING UP

THE PROCESS OF SETTING UP a restaurant dining room can be divided into two major parts: one is cleaning, and the other is preparing items (such as folded napkins) that will be consumed during service.

What needs to be cleaned? Everything that a guest might see! Of course, the floor staff needn't be responsible for the entire physical plant, but there are some parts that should fall under their supervision. Also, some objects that have been run through the dishwashing machine, although technically clean, might need to be steamed and/or polished. Here are some things that the floor staff should be responsible for:

- Silverware, both flatware and hollowware

- Glassware, especially wineglasses

- Menus and menu covers

- Gueridons and side stands

- Salt and pepper shakers

- All customer seating (chairs and banquettes)

- Front door glass and brass

- Mirrors and artwork in the room

- Tableside equipment: rechauds, salad bowls, decanters, duck presses, cheese-cutting contraptions, etc.

- Coffee station

- Bread warmers

The list could go on, but it's a good start. The waiters shouldn't be responsible for the whole restaurant, just the areas with which they have direct contact.

Consumable items other than plates of food need to be prepared for each service. There are both food and nonfood items belonging to this category, and they must be stocked up to a level that is appropriate for the amount of business expected for service. Some of these actions are as follows:

- Place folded napkins for guests (one at each place setting, with backups available at the side stand)

- Stock folded napkins at the bar for wine service

- Fill creamers with milk or half-and-half for coffee service

- Cut lemons for hot and iced tea

- Fill sugar bowls

- Fill salt and pepper shakers

- Prepare butter (curls or pats) for bread service

- Line bread baskets with napkins and fill baskets with bread

- Load up side stands with flatware for marking (setting) tables for subsequent courses

This too is a list that could be added to, depending on the needs of the particular establishment. The most important thing to do when creating these setup lists is to be exhaustive in seeking out the things that need to be done, but remain flexible as to their priority and how often they need to be done. The salt shakers have to be full for every service, but you only have to dust the moose head's antlers once a week.

BREAKING DOWN

I'VE NEVER MET AN EMPLOYEE who enjoyed breaking down. The process of breaking down brings with it a unique problem: the staff wants to get out of there and might try to take some shortcuts. Proper supervision is the key here.

As with setting up, there are two major parts to consider: cleaning up the mess, and leaving the room ready for the next service staff that comes in to set up. The cleaning that needs to be done is different from that done during setup, and not really as much fun. Here is a partial list of details that need attention:

- Clean the coffee station (this can get nasty on a busy night)

- Empty crumbs from bread warming drawers

- Clean side stands (which also can get ugly)

- Stow bags of dirty linen for pickup

- Empty and wash creamers

- Empty garbage cans in the front of the house

- Clean food off tableside equipment

With regard to the second part of breaking down, setting up for the next service, there isn't quite as much to do, but it is notoriously difficult to get a tired, spent staff to do things that will make life easier for the next bunch coming in. In fact, in our business there is a grand tradition of one staff hating the staff from the previous shift. The vicious cycle begins when the lunch crew forgets to do some aspect of breakdown. The dinner shift then conveniently "forgets" to do something else to revenge the original misstep, and the war begins. The answer is, of course, for the manager to do a complete check of sidework at the end of the meal period, using a checklist that is an abbreviated version of the breakdown sheets and doing a physical check of every item on it. Asking the waiters if they took out the recyclables is not enough—the manager has to look inside the bin ("Oh, you meant *those* recyclables").

MANAGING THE LISTS

AS YOU MAY HAVE SURMISED, having a list (as good as it may be) is not enough. The administration of these setup and breakdown procedures is what ensures that the work is being done. This management of the process involves more than just babysitting the staff—the process itself must be under constant scrutiny as well. For example, you may find that the pantry is never set up on time for lunch

EXAMPLE OF DETAILED PANTRY SETUP LIST

- ☐ On the bottom shelf of the warmer, store the coffee cups for service and the teapots.
- ☐ Pick up the order from the storeroom at 8:30–9:00 a.m. Bring all up to the dining room.
- ☐ After cleaning out the lowboy, stock the storeroom order in the lowboy (first in, first out).
- ☐ All paper products go in the cabinet underneath the ice cream machine or in the long room on the designated shelf. Make sure this shelf is organized.
- ☐ Clean the two shelves where the sugar caddies are kept and then fill the sugar bowls and sugar substitute packet holders.
- ☐ Curl enough butter every day to fill two sheet trays two high of butter caddies, then fill a bain-marie with ice water and curl enough butter to fill—usually around 3–4 pounds of butter per day.

- ☐ Cut six lemons into wedges; do not forget to remove any brand-name stickers or stamps, the white center, and the seeds. Please score to fit easily onto glasses.
- ☐ Brew two gallons of iced tea every day. Allow to steep and then ice down in an ice bath and store in plastic water pitchers in lowboy. Do not put ice into tea. Throw out leftover iced tea at the end of the day.
- ☐ Line all bread baskets with serviettes and stack until right before service, when they are filled. Return the bread rack to the bake shop following service.
- ☐ Line all large silver runner trays with serviettes and stack on pantry station.
- ☐ Clean and organize the pantry station after completing opening duties.
- ☐ Please *do not* make coffee; runners will make coffee throughout service.

service, no matter who is doing the job. In that case it's likely that there is just too much work for one person to do, and some of the tasks should be given to other members of the staff. A side benefit of this reassessment process, beyond the increase in efficiency, is that the staff recognizes your desire to streamline operations, and will often respond with a stronger work effort—when they see that you care, it can have a positive effect on their work ethic.

A well-thought-out set of sidework sheets backed up by solid management is one of the best ways to ensure that the mundane tasks of setting up and breaking down the dining room will remain, mercifully, mundane.

SMALL SHINY OBJECTS

WHILE MOST OF THE CHORES THAT need to be done in the dining room are pretty much self-evident, there are some tricks with regard to glassware and flatware polishing that can move things along a bit more quickly.

First of all, why do glasses and flatware need to be polished anyway, since they just came out of the dishwasher? In a perfect world they would be shiny and ready to go, but realistically, water spots may mar their appearance, and occasionally some soil may remain. (You don't want a gentleman guest pointing out to you that the lipstick on the glass isn't his shade.) On top of that, there is nothing like having perfectly polished glasses and flatware on the table—you can almost *feel*, not just see, the difference in the appearance of the whole room. Shiny glasses, individual salt and pepper shakers, knife rests—little things can add up to big impressions for your guests.

Glasses should be steamed and then polished with a polishing cloth. Linen companies will rent these cloths to you, and they should be lint-free. As for the steaming, if there are lots of glasses to do, set up a chafing dish with a small amount of water in the hotel pan, then a shallow perforated pan set inside it. Place the glasses upside down on the perforated pan and allow the steam to collect inside the glasses and around the outside (also make sure that the bottom of the glass gets steamy, which can be accomplished by placing a napkin or polishing cloth over the assembled glasses). When the glasses are steamed up, take the base of the glass in one corner of the polishing cloth. Take the other end of the polishing cloth and stuff it into the bowl of the glass. Hold the base of the glass with one hand, and with the other hand stick your thumb into the bottom of the glass, with your fingers pointed toward the bottom as well. Begin to polish the glass by rotating it in the cloth, slowly moving your thumb and fingers up the side of the glass towards the lip. Because the base of the glass stays inside the cloth, the entire glass is now polished and can be placed back into a clean, dry glass rack, ready for use.

For smaller numbers of glasses, a water pitcher or some other vessel can be filled with boiling water to be used as a source of steam. While polishing, special care must be taken to check the glasses before and after for water spots, lipstick, and other soil.

Flatware doesn't show inadequate cleaning as clearly as glassware does, but try to remember what it feels like to see a piece of rice in a fork's tines or a fingerprint on the blade of a knife when you're eating in a restaurant. As with glasses, the flatware could be fresh from the dishwashing machine, but that extra-clean grain of rice in the fork still looks nasty. Polishing flatware is quicker than steaming glasses, but there are also some tricks here. It helps to have the different pieces separated before starting, which can actually start at the dish dropoff area by having waiters and bussers use a flatware separator bin. If not, do it before polishing because it speeds the process. A handful of flatware can be dipped into some hot water and then held inside a polishing cloth. Each piece should then be pushed through the fingers holding the cloth and into a clean, dry container (or separator) that will hold it until needed for use. As with the glasses, the flatware can be polished without any skin contact.

If the staff needs to count out large numbers of flatware pieces, they should use a scale. To do this, weigh twenty forks in a container that will fit on a kitchen scale. Do the same with each type of flatware and create a chart that shows what standard numbers of pieces weigh. If you know what a hundred forks weigh and you need four hundred for the banquet, don't count them out one by one—use the scale!

Whatever methods are used to do it, the sparkling clean glasses and flatware on the tables not only are noticeable to the guests but also provide an almost subconscious backdrop of cleanliness that guests can feel.

PERFECT TABLES

WALK INTO MOST RESTAURANTS AND you will find a clean place. It's expected. Yet there are some restaurants that just *feel* clean the minute you walk in. Some of it is, of course, the fact that the place really is spotless. The final touch, though, is the precision with which the dining room is set up, with everything in its place.

Large-scale precision starts with the placement of dining tables in the room. They should be in straight lines and evenly spaced, with the tables square to the wall. One more thing to do while arranging the tables is to make sure that the wait staff can get around and between all of the tables, so that every customer in the room can be served. This last step doesn't add to the look of the room, but it sure makes service go more smoothly.

TABLE LINENS CAN BE THE BANE of a restaurant manager's existence. High-quality napkins and tablecloths are not inexpensive to rent, with napkins ranging from pennies to dimes apiece, and tablecloths up to a dollar each. So every time a four-top sits down, it has already cost you two bucks! Sometimes linen is delivered that is either soiled, damaged, or in some other way unusable. If you don't separate it and return it for credit, you might as well be throwing dollar bills into the dirty linen bag. Lastly, service staff members are usually unaware of the costs involved with linen and will do things such as mopping up a spill with tablecloths, which is both expensive and unnecessary. The answer is diligence. Management must take the linen program seriously, training the staff to handle linen properly and maintaining the inventory just as they would any other consumable item in the restaurant, such as food or beverage. Don't give up control of a controllable.

In fancier restaurants, the next step is dressing the table with linen. It's a good idea, even with padded tables, to use an underliner of some sort, then a tablecloth on top. The underliner adds a sumptuous feel to the table both by padding the surface and by hanging a bit lower than the top cloth. Because larger tablecloths cost more to rent, you can save some money by using a slightly smaller tablecloth on top and changing the underliner only when it becomes soiled. Another option is to have underliners custom-made out of a darker fabric. These don't need to be cleaned as often, and though not cheap, they can cost less in the long run because you own rather than rent them.

With a nice clean tablecloth (or place mat, or fresh butcher paper) on the table, we're ready for the place setting. Whatever that means for a particular restaurant, there should be standards as to where its elements are placed on the table. One of the easiest things to do is to pick a simple measurement and stick to it. An inch from the edge of the table works well, or perhaps the width of a dinner knife—something that the wait staff can reproduce on a regular basis. The show plate or napkin should be centered at the diner's place, and all equipment should be placed around it. The specific pieces of flatware being set on the table are determined by the service style, and by what food will be served first. If an *amuse-bouche* is going to be served, for instance, there might be nothing besides the show plate and a cocktail fork.

Whatever the place setting consists of, create standards. Decide that the water glass should be placed one inch above the tip of the dinner knife. Salt and pepper shakers (or grinders), flower vases, candleholders, and the like should have their own places on each table. With the tables lined up and then set in this fashion, everything just feels right. The custom is to place chairs at the edge of the table (or tablecloth), not push them under the table.

TIP: When setting large or round tables for five or more guests, place the chairs evenly around the table before setting it. At a round table with an even number of diners, each seat should be directly across the table from another seat. With an odd number, the chairs should form a multipointed star. By placing the chairs before setting the table, you are guaranteed even spacing between the place settings (and guests).

I'm sure that there are some skeptics out there saying, "Why should I bother to make the dining room perfect when it's just going to get messed up by the guests anyway?" Well, why cut the vegetables into a perfect brunoise when they're just going into a ravioli filling? First of all, perfection for perfection's sake is a state of mind that pervades everything that you do. Not only does it define who you are and what you do, it also spreads throughout the staff, and therefore the restaurant. There's one more reason to do it, though. The one person who notices that the vegetables in the ravioli were perfect one-eighth-inch cubes and who sees that all of the water glasses in the room are lined up is the very same person we *want* to impress.

CHAPTER 5:
SERVING GUESTS:
THE MAIN EVENT

Okay, here we go. There are some people walking with intent from the parking lot toward the front door, and there's a good chance that they are your first guests of the evening. Since working the door has been explained in Chapter 3, we'll pick it up right as the guests are heading into the dining room.

The host or maître d' helps ladies and gentlemen with their chairs and wishes them a good meal. Menus can be distributed to the guests either by the person seating them or by their waiter. If the number of guests is fewer than the number of place settings, the maître d' should indicate this to the captain or waiter with a predetermined signal, such as placing the butter knife on top of the folded napkin, so that the waiter can remove the extra place settings. The wine list can accompany the menus, or it can be brought over by the waiter or captain. Personally, I like for the wine list to come separately—it's a good way for the captain or waiter to break into the conversation, it helps the staff to identify who the host of the table is, and it brings some attention to the list, influencing the guests to look at it and perhaps order from it. When the wine list is delivered with the menus, it can be overlooked, but handing it directly to one of the guests will initiate the ordering process.

THE FIRST SALE

THE GUESTS HAVE JUST SAT DOWN. Their server comes over, welcomes them to the restaurant—then invites them to spend some money! The first sale usually involves a beverage. I've found that a useful phrase is "Would you care for ice water or bottled water?" which I much prefer to the now ubiquitous "Bottled water or tap water?" It doesn't hurt sales, either—bottled-water drinkers will order it no matter what.

Once water preference has been determined, the captain or front waiter can move on to the drink order. (Mind you, the water and drink orders can be interchanged. In fact, taking the drink order first can help increase sales because it is likely the guests are thirsty from the trip to your place.) A polite, direct question such as "Would you like an aperitif or something else to start off with?" can be accompanied with a description of the house aperitif, drink special, or even a simple suggestion that they start off with a glass of sparkling wine or Champagne.

After the drinks are ready, they should be delivered to the table. This is the perfect time to let the guests know of any specials, changes, or items that the kitchen has run out of. It also allows the guests to mull over the menu with a drink in hand.

THE HABIT OF OPENING MENUS before handing them to the diners is somewhat controversial. It doesn't take a lot of effort for the guests to open the menu themselves, but it's a thoughtful touch. Still, think about how much money was spent on the design and printing of the menu covers. Handing the closed menu to the guests allows them to admire the lovely artwork or logo on the cover, and it also adds another visual memory to the diners' experience. When they think about the restaurant, there will be more than just food and service memories. Obviously, whether or not the menus are opened for the guest is part of the house style. If you're going to open them, though, maybe you should leave the outer cover blank to save some money.

READING THE GUEST

PROFESSIONAL SERVERS CAN TUNE IN to guests' desires and needs without needing to be a mind reader or asking brusque questions. For example, to find out how much help the guests will need with their menu selection, the waiter can ask, "Have you dined with us before?" If the guest answers no, the waiter knows that the guest might have to be coached through the ordering process. With repeat customers, the waiter can move on to recommendations and the order itself. A series of carefully phrased questions can garner some clues about what the waiter can suggest to the table that will both make them feel attended to and generate sales for the restaurant. For example, an initial dialogue might run as follows:

Q: Would you like to see our cocktail menu?

A: No, thanks, we'll just be drinking wine tonight.

Q: How about a wine list, then?

A: Sure, but we're not sure what we're going to be eating yet.

Q: May I suggest, then, a glass of Champagne while you make up your minds?

A: That sounds perfect!

The waiter followed the lead of the customers, guiding them toward a decision that would make them happy *and* be a nice sale for the house.

Of course, every guest is different, preferring different amounts of interaction with the staff. Some want to be left the heck alone, while others will keep you at the table all night. It is the job of a professional server to figure out what will make a guest happy—not just with regard to food and beverage but also in terms of the amount of interaction or familiarity.

TIPS ON READING GUESTS

IF THE GUESTS ORDER QUICKLY AND ACT ANXIOUS, they might be in a hurry. Ask them if they are and, if so, suggest items that don't take long to cook, as well as alert the kitchen. The opposite case is when guests want to take their time. This can be sensed when the guests order drinks and don't even open the menus for a while. In this case, the waiter should be patient and let the guests take their time. I have noticed over the years that pushing such guests to order is not a great thing to do; even though the guests might finish and leave earlier (allowing for a turned table), the guests, feeling rushed, will probably spend less money, and they may not come back. The people who linger often end up spending more money because they're sitting there longer.

I ASKED PAUL MCLAUGHLIN, general manager of Oceana in New York City, "Is reading guests an inborn talent?" He answered, "No, I don't think it is at all. I think you can actively read guests by focusing, and being there and watching them. I remember at Le Bernardin when smoking was still legal in the dining room, any time a woman would make a little break for her purse, I always knew that she was either going to get up and go to the ladies' room or go for a smoke. So, as soon as I saw that, I would be right at the table waiting for either one of those to occur." He added, "I think being in your station, watching the table, watching people eat, making eye contact to see what the body language is, is how you can accurately read a guest. Now, once you step off the floor and go into the back to try to sneak a cup of coffee, or go to the men's room at the wrong time . . . you know, if you step off the floor for a minute or two, you've missed something. You have to be watching. You have to be paying attention. You have to be looking. You have to be reading the table."

SUGGESTING VERSUS RECOMMENDING

MORE OFTEN THAN NOT, customers will have questions about the menu for the waiter to answer. Indeed, they usually want some advice from the waiter as well. One of the reasons for going to a restaurant in the first place is that a knowledgeable server can help the guest to order an enjoyable meal, recommending, for example, an appetizer that complements the main course particularly well (or helping diners avoid a combination that will clash), or suggesting a wine that will enhance what's been ordered.

When answering the guests' questions, the waiter has two choices: suggest or recommend. Suggesting is the safer of the two. For the most part, it consists of listing information without any personal opinion. For example:

Guest: "What white wines do you have by the glass?"

Waiter: "Well, we have Grüner Veltliner and Rkatsiteli."

Nothing personal here, just an offering of what is available. By not stating any opinions, the waiter is not personally responsible if the guest is unhappy with her glass of Rkatsiteli (assuming that she was able to pronounce the name). When it comes to food, the act of suggestion can go further than just naming the dishes— the staff's menu knowledge should be good enough that the ingredients and preparation techniques used in each dish can be recited. This can work in a lot of situations at the table, and it is relatively safe.

Life isn't always safe, though, and at some point the waiter will probably have to wade into the dangerous waters of personal recommendation. When the guest asks, "Which shellfish appetizer should I have?" the waiter can't just keep reciting the menu offerings over and over. No, the waiter is eventually going to have to offer an opinion, at which point he or she is vulnerable to blame for recommending something the guest finds less than satisfactory. However, the more time that a staff member spends working with a menu, or even a chef, the more he or she learns how customers react to different dishes, and can use that accumulated experience to make personal recommendations that almost always pay off. With this knowledge, it's not just the ingredients or even the preparation methods that the staffer can now describe, but the subtleties and even the personality of the dish.

The server's confidence is reassuring to the guest, increasing the level of emotional comfort at the table. When I recommend a bottle of wine to a table, the guests often ask me if I'm sure they're going to like it. My standard answer is, "If you don't like it, I'll drink it with *my* dinner." With this response, the guests know not only that I like the wine enough to drink it myself, but also that I will stand behind the recommendation. (Of course, use of this line should usually be restricted to management—it could be problematic in the hands of every single member of the wait staff.)

One of the tricks to use when coming up with suggestions is to mention a specific item to a guest to see how he or she reacts. For instance, you can bring up some unique characteristic of the dish, such as intense spiciness, wild mushrooms, or raw fish, and observe the guest's reaction. If he or she seems to register abject fear, it's time to pull back to a meat-and-potatoes position.

When the guest asks a question, the answer can be either information or an opinion. To decide which one to use, remember:

Suggestion = Safe

Recommendation = Risky

THERE ARE TWO CATEGORIES OF RUDE SURPRISES that guests don't like. One is unexpectedly raw food. Anytime a dish (especially one involving animal protein) is served raw, the waiter must tell the guest. Many times, I've had guests who thought that "tartare" was the sauce that comes with fish sticks. The other unpleasant shock can be mystery meat. Game and organ meats are notorious for frightening the uninitiated. As cute as that little grouse looks on the plate, for example, its flavor is intense.

ORDER TAKING

THE USUAL SIGN OF BEING READY TO ORDER is that the guests close their menus. Not every diner in America knows this, so the waiter needs to keep an eye on the table for other signs of readiness, such as looking around the room.

The waiter should approach the table and stand in a spot where the guests don't have to crane their necks in order to make eye contact. At a table for two, where the guests face each other, one of the empty sides is good. At a four-top, one of the corners between two guests is the best place to stand. It's permissible for the waiter to move around the table in order to hear the guests more clearly, but keeping unnecessary movement to a minimum is less distracting to the diners. If the guests don't immediately react to your presence, it's okay to wait for a lull in their conversation, then say, "If you'll pardon me for a moment, would you care to order?" or some such thing. Just don't interrupt right before the punch line of a joke.

Depending on the type of establishment, the most appropriate way for the waiter to stand is erect, with a slight bend at the waist (toward the customers). Some casual restaurants use the quarterback's one-knee-in-the-huddle position, or even have the server sit down at the table with the guests. This breaks down the professional/personal barrier by physically bringing the server to the guest's level. Personally, I'm not so hot on it, but it works for a lot of places.

PROTOCOL

Protocol is a set of rules that determines who gets served (or asked for an order) first at a table. The most practical application of protocol in modern restaurants would be to take care of children first (it quiets them down), then ladies, then gentlemen. To be even more proper, one would serve the children, then the older women, the younger women, the older gentlemen, and then the younger gentlemen, though this level of detail is not easy and not always possible.

THE ORDER

This is one of the most critical times in the meal—getting the order correct. The waiter should take the order from one person at a time, giving that guest devoted attention. The norm is to take the full order (all savory courses) from one person,

WHILE CLASSIC PROTOCOL INCLUDES ROYALTY, most of us don't need to know how to deal with a king or princess. But it could happen. One evening at Campagna, we had the pleasure of serving Prince Albert of Monaco. As we were placing the first few appetizers on the table, the prince's assistant leaned over to me and said, "Could you please serve His Highness first?" I was nonplussed, thinking that the ladies should be served first. Then I remembered about the use of classic protocol, with royalty being served before anyone else, and my confusion slowly turned to an appreciation of tradition in the old school of manners.

Guides that I've found useful for the finer points of etiquette and protocol include Mary Jane McCaffree's Protocol: *The Complete Handbook of Diplomatic, Official, and Social Usage* and Letitia Baldrige's books on manners and etiquette.

then move on to the next. It is acceptable to take the order for everybody's appetizers, then start over with main courses, but this method can lead to confusion on the part of both server and guest. As the server takes the orders, it is imperative that he or she confirms the order with each guest by repeating back the choices. In fact, it might be even better to repeat the order using an alternative name for the dish to avoid confusion. For example, the guest says, "I'll have the scallop main course." The waiter might then say, "So that will be the Sautéed Sea Scallops," just in case the customer perhaps meant the Escalope of Veal. Clearing up any potential confusion must be done now, rather than allowing the wrong menu item to be prepared and delivered to the table. One simple question while taking the order can avoid a big problem down the road.

The waiter should take the menus from the each guest after he or she orders. Once all of the orders are taken, the waiter has another chance to clear up any potential confusion. If some guests have ordered two courses while others have ordered three, this should be pointed out to the guests so they can either modify their orders to match each other's or at least be prepared for awkward moments when only a few members of the party will have food in front of them. If there is even a glimmer of doubt in the waiter's mind when he or she goes to put the order in, it is imperative to go back to the table to clear up that doubt before the kitchen starts work on it.

PLACING THE ORDER

The near ubiquity of point-of-sale (POS) systems has changed the way waiters take orders. Handwriting is not as important as it used to be, there is no longer any need for "cocktail shorthand," and waiters don't have to go into the kitchen anymore (which most chefs are glad for). However, the existence of such systems means that communication between front and back is more important than ever, and waiters have to send a lot of clear, accurate information to the cooks. Along with solid training on the computer system in use, waiters have to realize how important the process of placing the order is. The attitude of "Oh, I'll just put the order in, then go back to the kitchen to clear it up" is an example of haste that will definitely lead to waste. If the order is clear and free of errors, the server can push that send button and then move on to other chores. An unclear or mistake-riddled order, however, will require the attention and talents of the expediter, the waiter (who now has to go into the kitchen), and potentially the chef, manager, bartender, or cashier, none of whom have time to spare on such matters. What a mess! The irony is that just a few more moments is all it takes to make the order unmistakably clear. I tell my staff that they need to take their time and concentrate while at the computer. I also use the carpenter's motto: measure twice, cut once.

SOME SERVERS SEEM TO FEEL that going back to the table to clear up some uncertainty about the order makes them appear stupid or foolish. Instead of asking the guest questions that will clear everything up, the server would rather put the order in and see what happens. Not only is this a sure way to create unnecessary lapses in service, it is also a waste of time (to fix everything) and money (wasted food and labor). It is important that staff know that they are being more professional by clearing things up.

SEQUENCE OF SERVICE

1. Greeting
2. Seating
3. Bread
4. Beverage
5. Menu, wine list
6. Order taking
7. Serving
8. Clearing
9. Check presentation, payment
10. Farewell
11. Reset table

SEQUENCE OF COURSES

1. Appetizer
2. Soup
3. First course (may be a combination of the above items; also, a family restaurant may offer a choice of appetizer, soup, or salad as a starter course rather than as separate courses.)
4. Main course
5. Salad (traditionally served after the main course in a European-style meal; American restaurants generally serve salad between the soup and main course)
6. Fruit and cheese (usually offered only by fine-dining restaurants and some bistros)
7. Dessert
8. After-dinner (hot) beverages

CARRYING STUFF AROUND

I SOMETIMES DEFINE DINING room service as "carrying stuff around." It can sound a little irreverent, but when you think about it, hospitality is all about being nice to people, and you can be nice to people by bringing them stuff they're really going to enjoy. The basics of service are just that—the founda-

tion. Simple activities such as carrying plates or glasses need to be perfected to a point of automaticity so the waiter need not concentrate on them. When basic skills are perfected, they recede into the background and the staff can concentrate on the finer points of service and hospitality. Here's how you can perfect the basic skills of the dining room.

PLATE HANDLING

When I first thought that I knew how to carry three plates in one hand, I was doing it in such a way that cut off the circulation to my left index finger, and it hurt . . . a lot. Not long thereafter, I learned the correct way, which allowed me to stay in the business without permanent disfigurement. This ability allows you to carry four plates at the same time (three with one hand and arm and the fourth in the other hand), meaning that you can serve a four-top without any assistance (see photos). The practice is usually not allowed in more formal restaurants, where each server will carry only one or two plates at a time, avoiding anything that resembles plate stacking. Carrying fewer plates both is more elegant and allows the staff to perform synchronized service, where the food is placed in front of all guests at the table at the same time.

PLATE CLEARING

Clearing of dirty plates is handled somewhat differently. In some settings, you can use the same method as above to pick up plates and deliver them to the dish room. There is also a method whereby the plate with the most uneaten food is picked up first in the left hand, then subsequent plates are stacked on the heel of the hand, balanced with the left ring finger or pinky. In some banquet or casual settings, it is permissible to scrape the uneaten food from the upper plates to the lower one, to allow for stacking. This practice is a bit unappetizing for the guests, so the waiter should turn away from the table to conceal the procedure, though because this makes the process visible to guests at other tables, the practice should be avoided in nicer restaurants. In formal restaurants, clearing is done the same way as delivery—no more than two plates at a time.

PLATE HANDLING

1. Hold a plate by resting its base on the index finger and gripping its edge with the thumb.

2. Add a second plate by sliding it under the first so its base is resting on the middle finger and the ring and pinky fingers can further support it by fanning them underneath.

3. Add a third plate, resting it on the wrist, forearm, and outer edge of the second plate.

DELIVERING FOOD ON TRAYS

- If the tray does not have a cork or nonskid surface, you can place a damp cloth napkin on the tray to prevent items from slipping.

- Place heavy items in the center of the tray and slightly toward the carrier. Place flatware and smaller items toward the outer edge of the tray.

- Avoid placing filled stemware near the edge of the tray; they are top-heavy and can fall off easily, especially when the waiter is going around a turn.

- Never stack cold food on top of hot food when plate covers are used. Heat travels upward and could warm the cold plate to possibly unhealthy temperatures.

- Place beverage hollowware (coffee pots, water pitchers) toward the center of the tray.

- Keep all objects within the boundaries of the tray. Items hanging over the edge can get knocked off more easily.

- Keep open plates containing food well away from the hair.

- Do not overstock or overfill trays. Get help or make additional trips. A tray should contain no more than six to eight plates with covers.

CLEARING WITH TRAYS

NO MORE THAN ONE TRAY should be placed on the tray stand; it's not easy to separate stacked trays when the top one is full. One solution is to invert all trays except the one on top. This way, the top (full) tray can be slid off and onto the server's carrying hand. The technique can add efficiency but should be done with care because the trays, if wet, can be slippery and slide off too easily.

Flatware should be separated by type to make it easier to sort in the dish room. Scraped plates should not be stacked more than five high (and no more than two stacks per tray). Heavy items should be placed near the middle of the tray, slightly closer to one of the long sides. This gives you a balanced tray with its center of gravity slightly to one side. The waiter will pick it up from the side that the plates are closer to so that carrying it is less awkward.

Empty bottles should be laid down so they won't fall over and possibly fall off the tray.

Full trays can be heavy. Care should be taken to avoid overfilling trays to reduce the number of trips to the kitchen, because an overloaded tray can bring on a trip to the emergency room instead. The server should always bend at the knee as he or she lifts the tray with the left hand above the left shoulder, but the tray should not rest upon the shoulder. While it may seem counterintuitive, it is better to use the fingertips to hold the tray rather than the open palm. While the latter may seem a stronger and more stable use of the hand, it doesn't allow for the finer adjustments possible with the fingers. Also, use of the open palm creates strain in the forearm that can lead to persistent pain. Of course, it takes a little time to build up strength in the carrying hand to enable waiters to carry trays on top of their splayed fingertips, but it's worth it.

The reason for trays to be carried above the left shoulder is that it frees the right hand for opening doors (you'll notice that most kitchen doors swing that way) and keeps the weight close to the server's center of gravity. The server should pick up full trays with a straight back, in sort of a genuflecting position. The tray should also be put down with a straight back by kneeling down next to the tray stand or dish room sorting area.

GLASSWARE

Stemware should be handled by the stem, and other glasses should be handled as close to their bases as possible. Also, fingers should never be placed inside any glass, clean or dirty. The first reason is to avoid putting fingerprints on the sides of the glasses. The second is that carrying dirty glasses with your fingers inside them may imply to the guest that this is how clean glasses are handled as well, which is unsanitary.

THE TEN RULES OF RESTAURANT SAFETY

Safety is serious. Don't take chances with your own or others' welfare.

1. If you see a spill or broken glass on the floor, alert those around you and either stay there yourself to warn others or get someone else to do so until it is cleaned up.

2. If a guest has a handbag or some other personal object on the floor by the table, offer to move it or place it in the coat check. Members of the floor staff might trip over it and hurt themselves or the guests.

3. Report all injuries to management, no matter how slight, and get immediate first aid.

4. Never run in the restaurant. It is easy to get hurt, or hurt someone else. Also, if guests see someone running, it can make them nervous, thinking that something might be wrong.

5. Use the correct doors into and out of the kitchen. When using the In door, go all the way in without stopping. There is a good chance that someone is right behind you walking just as fast as you are. By stopping in the doorway, you can both get hurt. Same goes with the Out door.

6. Avoid horseplay and practical jokes. Harmless fun can result in injury.

7. Report all defective equipment. Obey safety rules when you are working with any equipment.

8. Avoid backing up or making sudden, jerky movements.

9. Always wear shoes with nonskid soles.

10. Always store cleaning chemicals far away from any food products or serviceware.

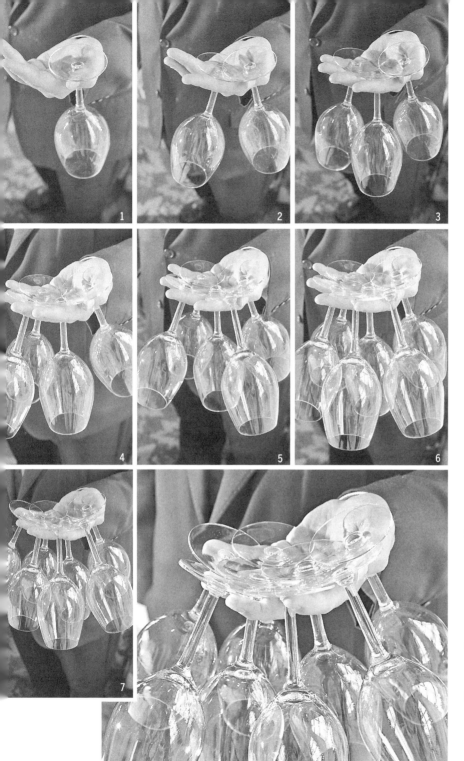

WAITER CARRYING WINE GLASSES

1. Turn the left hand palm upward. Place the stem of a glass between the index finger and thumb, so the glass is upside down and the base of the glass is resting on the fingers and palm of the hand.

2. Add the second glass between the index and middle fingers.

3. Add a third glass by placing it between the ring and pinky fingers.

4. Place a fourth glass between the ring and middle fingers.

5. The fifth glass is placed between the thumb and index finger. Be sure the glass already held there is held as far back as it can go. The fifth glass is secured additionally by placing its base under the bases of the first and second glasses.

6. Add a sixth glass between the index and middle fingers. Again, secure the glass by placing its base under the base of the glass already held in this position.

7. A seventh glass is added between the ring and pinky fingers.

8. An eighth glass is added between the ring and middle fingers. When adding the last few glasses, slightly flex the hand, curling the tips of the fingers slightly upward to better grasp the glasses.

As with plates, how you carry glasses depends on the type of restaurant. It is always safest to carry glasses on a bar tray, whether clean or dirty. Dirty glasses, of course, must be transported on a tray because there is often liquid still in them, and for the sake of efficiency. It can be appropriate to carry clean stemware hanging upside down between the fingers of your nondominant hand. I approve of this method in most restaurants because it promotes efficiency—at least eight glasses can be carried this way, and there is no tray to dispose of once the glasses have been placed on the table. However, in the most formal dining atmospheres, this practice might be frowned upon and a tray used instead.

FLATWARE

A waiter should touch only the handle of any type of flatware, clean or soiled. Flatware should always be transported on a clean tray or plate, usually on top of a folded, clean napkin. Some form of silverware transport plate (STP) should be used both for setting tables initially and for any replacement of serviceware for subsequent courses. It is unacceptable for a waiter to walk around the room with a fistful of forks and knives clinking and clanking. The use of a tray keeps the noise down and also allows for better organization by keeping the different types of flatware together. Other than aesthetics, delivering flatware from a tray or plate is faster than having to pick through a bundle of forks, knives, and spoons.

AS YOU MAY HAVE FIGURED OUT, the more formal a restaurant gets, the less you are allowed to carry at any one time. It's just more elegant to bring a single glass of wine over on a tray than to carry it by hand. It is more soigné to pick up just two dirty plates from the table and take them directly into the kitchen. It is feasible in such restaurants because as the prices go up, so does the staff-to-guest ratio. In a diner, where speed and low prices are desired, many fewer steps are performed for the guest, and "Keep your knife, hon" is the norm. As formality increases, there are more things to do for each guest, more staff to perform these steps, and higher prices to support the increased payroll.

STANDARDS OF SERVICE

WHILE EACH RESTAURANT HAS ITS OWN STYLE and way of doing things, there are certain standards that should be adhered to. Just about every restaurant should do the following:

- Greet guests within one minute of being seated.

- Serve children first, then older persons, first women and then men. Serving the kids first quiets them down; the rest is polite to do.

- When serving or clearing a table, always look where you are going. Never walk backward because you could trip over a guest's leg or chair, or back into a fellow staff person. Before turning around, look first to make sure there's no one behind you.

- Serve courses in the traditional sequence, unless otherwise specified or requested by the guest.

- Hot food hot, cold food cold.

- Ask the guest if they would prefer ice water or bottled water. Lemon or lime wedges can be offered, but are not assumed. Unless specifically requested, bottled water is served chilled without ice (the ice cubes are not made from the same water).

- Serve beverages from the right with the right hand.

- Remove soiled dishes from the right with the right hand, except bread-and-butter plates, which are picked up from the left. Do not scrape dishes in front of the guests.

- Avoid reaching across in front of a guest. If a guest's location makes this impossible, just apologize with a quick "Pardon my reach," then get it done. After a while, the guest might get tired of apologies, so read the guest to see if more are necessary or not.

- Do not clear plates until everybody at the table is finished with that course. By taking plates early, the folks who are still eating can feel uncomfortable and singled out. Just wait.

- Wait for the guest to ask for the final bill. Since some Americans don't know about this convention, if a guest seems ready for their check and doesn't ask, it is acceptable to say, "Would you like me to get your check for you?'

- Make sure someone is at the front door not only to greet incoming guests but to thank those on their way out.

- And the most important of all: be nice.

WHERE'S THE STUFF?

MOST RESTAURANTS have some form of serviceware storage in the dining room. It's usually called a side stand, and it holds items that the waiters will need during the course of service. It has space for enough flatware to make it through a night of setting and resetting tables, glassware for wine served by the bottle, folded napkins for guests who drop theirs, pepper mills, salt shakers, and cheese graters. Whatever the waiter needs on a momentary basis should be within a few steps of his or her station. I once worked in a restaurant that didn't have side stands, and having to go back to the kitchen for every little thing made for some very long evenings.

HANDLING PROBLEMS

IT'S GOING TO HAPPEN—something will go wrong. When it does, it's somebody's job to fix it. I'm not talking about the icemaker breaking down or a toilet backing up, both of which have happened in restaurants where I've worked. The problems I'm referring to are the ones that happen with regard to customers on a daily basis. Sometimes they're big, sometimes they're little, but either way they have to be dealt with. Problems tend to fall into one of several categories, which need to be addressed in different ways.

FOOD AND BEVERAGE PROBLEMS

Either there is something wrong with the product and it needs to be replaced, or the guest does not like it and it has to be replaced.

When a steak is gristly or the Champagne is flat, anyone can see that the product is not up to standard. Normal guest recovery procedures (see "Guest Recovery," page 102) can be followed, getting a replacement for the substandard item and perhaps doing a little something extra for the guest. It's not as easy when the guest is not happy with a perfectly good menu item or bottle of wine. Staff members can feel irritated or even angry when a guest complains about, say, a steak that to most observers is cooked perfectly. Unfortunately, *medium-rare* is a relative term, and the guest's perception is the truth in this case. No matter who explains that the meat is perfectly prepared, the customer will not be happy.

In the vast majority of cases when a guest is unhappy because what's on the plate or in the glass is not what he or she expected, the best solution is to apologize and then bring the guest something pleasing. I once spoke with a woman who told me that at a restaurant she'd ordered a salad with sweetbreads, not knowing that sweetbreads are the hypothalamus gland of a calf. What she was expecting was pieces of sweet *bread,* and when the dish arrived, her disappointment was strong enough that she didn't go back to that restaurant for a year. Looking at an incident such as this, it's possible to spot several places where such a problem could have been avoided. Obviously, the guest made an assumption about the menu item and didn't ask the waiter what sweetbreads were, but the waiter evidently didn't tell her, either, probably not wanting the guest to feel talked down to. The thing is, if the customer expects one thing and gets another, it doesn't matter how good the food that arrived at the table is. The sweetbreads might be the best dish on the menu, but the guest wasn't thinking "gland" when ordering.

Part of the solution is to write menus that are clear and easily understood. The other part is to have a staff that is capable of sensing a guest's uneasiness during the ordering process or spotting the potential for problems to arise with certain types of dish.

Whether real or perceived, guests' disappointment with the food that has been served to them must be dealt with swiftly. Disenchantment can turn into annoyance very quickly.

SOMETIMES PROBLEMS OCCUR because guests don't know what to expect. One of the dishes on the menu at the Hudson River Club was called Ice Plate of Chilled Seafood with a Tomato-Horseradish Sorbet. It was an assortment of shrimp, oysters, and clams served on a plate of ice, with what was essentially a frozen cocktail sauce. One evening a guest ordered it, enchanted by the idea of a plate made out of ice. The dish was delivered, but shortly thereafter the woman summoned over the captain (by banging a knife on her bread plate) and complained, "This sorbet is ice cold, and I'm surprised to find that in a restaurant of this caliber!" The captain, concealing a smile, said, "I'm terribly sorry, madam. Would you like me to have it heated up for you?"

I ASKED ANTHONY SCOTTO, of New York's Fresco by Scotto, what makes his place unique, and he immediately talked about his family being there: "Whatever it was, it was our family being present to make sure that it was being operated well. The nice thing about our family is that Elaina knows how to cook. And Rosanna, she knows how to cook. And it might be specific dishes, but they can make those specific dishes very well, which accounts for what we think people would want to have as a taste when they get to the table."

DINING ROOM CONDITIONS

One guest says it's too hot, but another thinks the same dining room is too cold. One guest says that the room is too noisy, while another says she can't hear the music well enough. Someone complains that the sun is in his eyes, and another person then summons the waiter to ask that the shade be lifted because she can't see the sunset.

There is no way to please everyone, but a couple of techniques will help you to get closer. One is to address common complaints before they happen, and the other is to pay attention to oft-repeated complaints about the dining room.

There are some situations that seem constant from restaurant to restaurant. Here are a few:

- Elderly guests tend to feel cold more easily than younger guests do. When possible, seat them away from any known drafts, and when that isn't possible, turn down the air-conditioning a bit.

- Most customers don't like to sit next to the swinging kitchen door. Either don't put a table right next to the door or, if you can't afford not to, at least face the table away from the door or make it a four-top; deuces are more easily distracted because fewer people are talking.

- Sitting next to the band or in front of the sound system can be unbearably loud for most guests. Nowadays, audio system designers tend to distribute a larger number of small speakers around the dining room, which allows for lower volume levels but still ensures that the music can be heard throughout the room.

- Dining rooms that are too dark make it hard to read the menu. Well-aimed lights over the tables or raising the overall light level somewhat will not only solve that problem but also make it easier to see the carefully presented food.

Every dining room has its own foibles, though, and listening for certain repeated complaints will help you to pinpoint specific problems that need your attention. Where I work, for instance, one of our tables is constantly vibrating. There is a large kitchen blower motor right under it, and some guests just hate it. The suggestion that they pretend they're dining on the Orient Express rarely appeases them. If a table of guests is not placated by apology and/or free food, the only choice is to move them to another table.

SERVICE ISSUES

Problems with service generally fall into one of two categories: a problem in the dining room or a problem in the kitchen. The guest, of course, sees no difference between the two, so no matter what, the onus is on the dining room staff to fix it, no matter where the problem really lies. There are many, many potential service problems, but here are some of the most common, with potential solutions.

Guests not getting enough attention	Stations need to be smaller Keep staff (or manager) in the dining room Hire new waiters
Food coming out too slowly	Change cooking procedures to allow quicker pickup of food Have waiters fire food earlier
Steps of service falling through the cracks	Redistribute responsibilities among dining room staff

Many service problems can be avoided if the manager or captain rarely leaves the dining room. The waiters are, because of the nature of their jobs, moving around the restaurant—picking up drinks from the service bar or running into the kitchen to find out if the soup is vegetarian. The best solution is to have someone whose main responsibility is to watch the room and the guests within it. In most cases, it should be a dining room manager, but in restaurants where the tip pool is big enough, you can add headwaiters or captains. Whereas some waiters might

SOMETIMES THE WAITER CAN FEEL CONFLICTED at the table: "Should I tell them that the Steak Tartare is raw, or will they feel as though I think they're stupid?" There can be clear signs that a guest needs to be clued in, especially when he or she orders that tartare well done. It usually isn't that obvious, though. This is when experience in reading guests comes in handy. A guest who shows the signs of being someone who dines out frequently (for example, someone who immediately takes the napkin and places it on his or her lap) probably doesn't need to be told that Vichyssoise is served cold. The diner who has less apparent dining experience (the napkin stays on the table) can be clued in subtly, though. One way is to repeat back their menu choice in a descriptive manner, such as "So you will start with the cold potato-leek soup, then move on to the chilled raw beef for dinner?" Without such clear indications, though, the waiter should look for signs of tension or confidence in their guests, and work to relieve the tense diner while perhaps taking the confident guest into more adventurous territory by suggesting things they might not have had before.

begrudge an extra person added to the tip pool, the smart ones realize that the captains can add to the pool by selling wine, upselling the menu, and providing more immediate service than the waiter is able to.

DELAYS

Anyone who has ridden a subway has been stuck on a train at some point and knows that the frustration of being in a stationary subway car in a dark tunnel can be relieved somewhat by hearing the conductor announce the reason for the delay and that the train will be moving shortly. The same holds true for restaurant patrons. When a guest has to wait a long time for anything, the waiter is aware of the problem but usually chooses to hide from the guest rather than face him or her. This, of course, adds to the guest's frustration. If the waiter instead goes directly to the guest and explains the delay, the guest, while still somewhat inconvenienced, usually relaxes a bit. In fact, saying something like "The chef wasn't happy with the quality of your main course and is preparing another one for you" can make the guest feel particularly well taken care of—it's nice to know that the chef is watching over you. The key here is, of course, for the waiter not to avoid the problem—it won't go away by itself.

GUEST RECOVERY

THE TERM *GUEST RECOVERY* implies that you had the guest at some point but lost him or her somewhere along the way, and in a way that's exactly what happens when there is a problem, whether it be with the food, the service, or the dining room environment. You can sense when it happens—everything is going along nicely, but then the guest gets the wrong food, or it's cold, or it takes too long, and the atmosphere at that table suddenly changes. Many waiters will avoid the guest at this point, apparently hoping that the problem will go away if they ignore it, but the only reliable way to get a customer back is to address the problem and the guest directly. Avoidance merely exacerbates the problem. When something has gone wrong, the best time to correct it is at the beginning, before the guest has had a chance to become annoyed or resentful.

For example, the cook leaves a steak under the broiler for too long, and the meat now looks like it could be carbon-dated. The kitchen immediately puts another steak on the grill, but it will take fifteen minutes to reach medium-well, as the guest requested. The waiter could at this point go to the guest, apologize for the anticipated delay, and perhaps bring the guest a little something to munch on during the wait. Or the waiter could avoid the guest altogether, figuring that the steak will eventually arrive. In the first case, the guest might be a little miffed but will at least know what is causing the long wait for dinner, and perhaps will be happy to get a little something free out of the deal. In the second case, the guest spends the next fifteen minutes darting annoyed glances around the room, wondering when the food is going to arrive. That fifteen minutes can seem like hours, putting the guest directly on the express to Grumpyland. So how do you bring the annoyed guest back?

APOLOGIZE

Apologizing is one of the easiest things to do, but too often the power of a simple apology is ignored in favor of much more elaborate schemes. When the slip-up is not too serious, sometimes an apology is all you need to appease the guest. The foundation of an effective apology is, of course, sincerity. To show sincerity, the server should:

- Make eye contact

- Use the words "I'm sorry"

- Avoid blaming others

Making eye contact is *not* the easiest thing to do. Eyes are indeed the windows to the soul, but not everybody wants to look in there. Even if you can't muster the courage to look straight into the eyes of someone who doesn't, for the moment, like you very much, saying you're sorry goes a long way.

Having apologized to the guest, blaming someone else for the slip-up can instantly bring into question the sincerity of the person doing the apologizing. Most guests realize that the waiter is not personally responsible for the undercooked chicken, but a server taking the blame can bolster the reputation of the entire staff.

CORRECT THE PROBLEM

There is a series of basic steps that are key to correcting any problem.

- **FIND OUT THE GUEST'S VERSION OF THE PROBLEM.** Don't assume you know what the guest is upset about. A veal chop that's still a bit pink in the center is not necessarily the problem—it could be the broccoli rabe that the guest wasn't expecting.

- **REMOVE THE OFFENDING ITEM.** If a caterpillar is doing the mambo across the mizuna, the sight of it will only upset the guest more—get it off the table right away.

- **TAKE STEPS TO REMEDY THE SITUATION.** Go directly to the person who can accomplish that. For example, if the manager or maître d' is the only person allowed to talk to the chef, then go find him or her—now.

- **GIVE THE GUEST AN ACCURATE TIME FRAME FOR THE REPLACEMENT.** Don't forget that when everybody else at a table has their food, an extra five minutes to bring a replacement for one of the guests can seem like a lot longer. Once the wheels have been set in motion to correct the problem, you should go to the guest to let him or her know how long it will take. An honest and accurate estimate will help you to build your credibility. Be conservative, that is, overestimate the time needed. If the replacement item comes out sooner than you said, the guest should be even happier.

- **BRING THE REPLACEMENT PERSONALLY, IF POSSIBLE.** First, it shows personal concern. Also, it allows the waiter to confirm the guest's satisfaction, or lack thereof, immediately. If a nameless, faceless runner brings the dish to the table, neither takes place.

MAKE IT UP TO THE GUEST

Here is where professional judgment and experience can really come into play. The most important thing to recognize is that there are different kinds of problems, of varying degrees of seriousness. There is no single answer to the question "What should I do to make the guest happy?" A few suggestions:

- Consider each situation on an individual basis.

- Don't always assume that offering a free dessert is the best solution.

- The response should match the situation in scale and nature.

Have you ever had a service problem in a restaurant and been offered dessert on the house as the waiter's attempt to appease you? What I call the "Band-Aid dessert" can sometimes have an effect opposite from the one desired. Before choosing a remedy to the situation, consider both the seriousness of the problem and the type of problem. For example, a guest's surprise that sweetbreads are actually from an animal is often not too serious and may well be taken care of with an apology, a replacement, and a free Danish, but when an entire dinner is ruined by interminable delays, the response needs to be different. Sometimes, when the meal has suffered a series of errors, it takes a grand gesture such as buying the whole dinner and inviting the guests back for another visit on the house, so they can see what the experience is supposed to be like. Consider the problem when finding a solution. If the guest is unhappy with a cocktail, a glass of wine chosen by the waiter to accompany the guest's next course is both more appropriate in style and closer in proximity to the problem than a free dessert at the end of the meal. Or if the guest complains that their appetizer was lackluster, you could send out a plate of risotto along with the main courses—the risotto that you overheard all the guests discussing, though nobody actually ordered it.

A guest is much more likely to be impressed by an action that shows both thought and consideration on the part of the waiter and management. While a free dessert is not the worst thing to get because of a mistake in service, it feels about as special as the socks and underwear you got on your last birthday—useful, but not very creative.

FOLLOW-UP

Arguably, follow-up is the most important part of the guest recovery process. You could carry out all of the previous steps, but all is for naught if the guest never gets the replacement steak or the drinks that you promised to buy are still on the check. Any goodwill that you engendered by offering to take care of the guest's bad experience is gone when the guest doesn't get what was promised.

The more often you carry out these steps in guest recovery, the more precise your judgments will be. Just think of it as the difference between knowing when you just have to apologize to your mate and when you need to buy flowers.

THE DIFFICULT GUEST

IN WRITING THIS BOOK, I have consciously avoided depicting guests in a negative light. After all, they are the reason why we, and everyone else we work with, have jobs. Yet there are times when a guest can become unreasonable or downright dangerous to himself, herself, or other guests. This has happened to me precious few times, for which I am thankful. But, statistically, it's going to happen to you at some point, and it helps to be ready for it.

First of all, if the behavior has a criminal aspect to it, call the police. Don't try to handle it yourself because you or your guests may get hurt. Second, if the safety or well-being of your staff is being threatened in any way, deal with the problem swiftly and without hesitation.

Certain situations will turn up more often than others, and here are a few of the most common.

DRUNKENNESS

The answer here is, of course, prevention. Your staff should be well trained with regard to responsible service of alcohol and must be aware of signs that a guest is becoming inebriated. Overserving is illegal and dangerous, and it must be avoided. If it happens, though, the drunken guest must be cut off from further service of alcohol. The process of doing so is never—I repeat, never—easy. Public embarrassment mixed with private shame do not a happy guest make. A direct, honest approach works best, especially if the staff member shows concern for the guest's safety. Offer the guest nonalcoholic beverages (on the house), get the guest's car keys, and maybe even arrange for a cab ride home. If the guest is belligerent, refuses help, and intends to drive home, warn the person that you will call the police, and then do so. You might save someone's life.

DISORDERLY CONDUCT

On occasion, a guest or group of guests will be making enough noise that other diners are disturbed by it. Sometimes the presence of a manager in the vicinity of the troublemakers is enough to quiet them down, but not always. Here again, prevention works best. Bachelor parties, victory celebrations, and surprise birthdays are events that can get a little rowdy, and steps can be taken to lessen their impact on the rest of the dining room. Housing the event in a private room is ideal, or it can be put in a separate or secluded part of the restaurant. If these options are not available, the host of the party should be made aware that appropriate behavior will be expected and that he or she will be responsible for it.

RUDENESS

Occasionally there will be a guest who is particularly rude to other guests, the staff, and/or the management. As professionals, we should expect to deal with a certain amount of this, but no guest should suffer at the hands of another diner. Any such behavior should be nipped in the bud, with the manager taking the brunt of the difficult guest's wrath. Similarly, the wait staff has enough to deal with already, and any extraordinary rudeness by a guest will often be enough to hurt service in the rest of a server's station. It is the manager's job to isolate and deal with a guest who is making trouble. Almost every time that I have asked a guest to leave the premises, I have absorbed the check—it's a good investment because, if nothing else, the miscreant will be leaving sooner.

RESPONSIBILITY TO THE GUEST

In the spirit of true hospitality, our doors are open to anyone who chooses to dine with us. We are, by definition, vulnerable to the good, bad, and indifferent behavior of the public, but we have a responsibility to all of our guests to make them feel attended to. It's one of the things that intensify the positive feelings that we reap, and adds to the honorability of our profession.

CHAPTER 6:
TABLESIDE
COOKING

The practice of tableside preparation of food has been around for a long time, partly because it's a very special experience. Think of a dessert prepared at your table: the warmth of the flame on your face, the combination of cold, warm, and sweet in your mouth. There are few other things we can do in the restaurant industry that are more impressive, or ultimately as satisfying, as cooking in the dining room.

There is a business side to this as well. First of all, cooking (or finishing, or carving) food in the dining room can take some of the load off a busy station in the kitchen. Believe me, when the expediter calls out "two Bananas Foster" to the pastry station, there is often a sigh of relief from the pastry cooks because all they have to do is put a couple of bananas and ramekins with butter and sugar into a copper pan and send it out. No sauce painting, no broken tuiles.

The other business-related reason is strictly monetary. Simply put, you can charge more money for tableside items. The cost of ingredients for a Caesar Salad is the same whether it's made in the kitchen or at the table, but you can charge more for that salad when it's prepared in front of the guests, because of the added show.

The excitement and satisfaction of the guest, of course, can lead to the financial success of a restaurant is less obvious ways. Return business and word of mouth are hard to measure, but both are sure to increase as you boost the value perceived by the guests. Performing some food preparation in the dining room can be a valuable tool in that regard.

THE SHOW

COOKING IN FRONT OF GUESTS IS SCARY. It's hard enough to wait tables as it is, and now guests are watching intently as the waiter works with a sharp knife to prepare the food and causes flames to shoot up from a copper pan. The only way to assuage the fear is experience: as the waiters repeat the preparation over and over, they will become more comfortable with it—and maybe even be able to enjoy the showmanship involved.

Tableside preparation can be appropriate to several types of establishment—it's not just the province of the most formal French restaurants. In fact, a casual eatery might be a great place to introduce flaming after-dinner coffees, which could increase sales. The staff must be trained and coached through the process, but if it works, more items can gradually be added. Start slowly, and see how both the staff and the guests react.

THE EQUIPMENT

THE AMOUNT OF MONEY SPENT on equipment depends on which dishes are going to be prepared. At a bare minimum, say for a cold salad, the waiter needs a flat, stable surface at a convenient height, as well as the small equipment to prepare the dish. With the move to more complex preparations and hot food, the need for specialized equipment increases. Here are some items that you should be familiar with when entering into the world of tableside preparation:

- **GUERIDON.** Here's that flat, stable surface! Originally, the word *gueridon* referred to a small table meant to hold a lamp or vase, supported by a tall column or sculpture of a human or mythological figure. However, in modern dining rooms the gueridon is a rolling trolley with a few shelves—the bottom ones used for storage of equipment and flatware, the top as the work surface. I have also seen the use of small, movable tables in some dining rooms, most notably at Restaurant Paul Bocuse near Lyon in France, and I liked the homey touch. Gueridons with wheels, though, are more convenient if you only have one or two for the whole restaurant and they need to be highly mobile.

- **SALAD BOWL.** A good-sized unfinished wooden salad bowl is used for Caesar Salad as well as other tableside salads. Unfinished wood is the material of choice because its mildly rough surface allows the waiter to crush the garlic and anchovy filets into a paste that will dissolve into the dressing. A smooth-surfaced bowl would leave chunks of garlic and anchovy in the dressing, which could be jarring to the palate.

- **RECHAUD.** The term *rechauffer* means "to reheat" in French, and the rechaud is a heating unit or burner that is used to heat up or cook food in the dining room. Fuel sources vary, the most old-fashioned being alcohol. Canned heat came into favor later, but the current most popular choice is the portable butane or propane burner. There are equipment companies that make attractive metal holders that hide the workmanlike burners from the guests' view. Also available are gueridons that have refillable butane burners built in. These trolleys are not inexpensive, but their sleek appearance adds a soigné touch to the dining room.

- **COPPER PANS.** Any cooking that will take place in the dining room should be done in attractive cookware. Copper is the most traditional and (in my opinion) most attractive metal surface for the exterior of any sauté pans to be used in the dining room. Copper is also an excellent conductor of heat and will shorten the amount of time required to preheat the pan for any cooking application. Bimetal pans have a stainless-steel or tin interior surface that is bonded to the copper exterior. A stainless lining is more durable and more common these days; a tin lining will eventually wear away, and the pan will

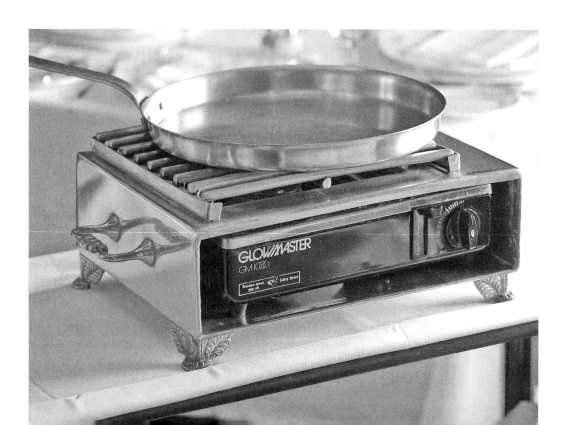

have to be retinned. For many applications, most notably fish (both flat and round), an oval pan is usually best. However, the traditional Crêpes Suzette pan is a wide, round, shallow pan that allows the whole crêpe to be coated in sauce before it is folded into its serving shape.

- **ZABAGLIONE PAN.** One of the easiest tableside desserts is Zabaglione (warm, whipped egg yolks with sugar and Marsala wine) served over fresh fruit. It is usually prepared in a hemispherical solid copper pan with a handle. The cooking is done over a rechaud or sterno as in the photo above.

- **CAFÉ DIABLO SET.** The dramatic coffee preparation Café Diablo requires a pan similar to a Zabaglione pan, with a stand that holds the pan over a heat source so that the waiter can use both hands during the preparation.

- **MISCELLANEOUS SMALL EQUIPMENT.** Cutting boards, carving knives, boning knives, pepper mills, soup tureens, and ladles are needed for various tableside dishes and must be in good working condition (knives sharp, for instance) as well as attractive. Also, the serving spoon and fork from your flatware pattern should be the same length, to make one-handed service of food easier.

THE FOOD

WHEN PREPARING FOOD IN THE DINING ROOM, we can't stick our fingers in the sauce to taste it, or pop a crouton in our mouths, or even poke a steak with a finger to determine doneness. With regard to seasoning, there are two ways to deal with this limitation. One is to use ingredients that are inherently salty or well seasoned to begin with, such as anchovies, Parmigiano Reggiano cheese, Worcestershire sauce, and prepared mustard. The other way to ensure well-seasoned food is to send some of the mise en place to the dining room preseasoned. The demiglace can have some salt in it from the get-go. This approach, of course, requires a high level of trust in the kitchen staff.

Doneness of meat or fish is perhaps an even thornier problem. Any checking by touch has to be done with the serviceware, but the most important factor is the amount of experience that the waiter has had preparing the dish. Uniformity of portion size is important here. The filets for Steak Diane should be pounded to the same thickness every time, and the size of fish should stay within a narrow range. This will help to make cooking times similar. Whoever is doing the preparation should have a chance to practice the dish at least once before making it for a guest. In fact, the waiter should be allowed to sample the dish after cooking it so that he or she knows what it should taste like; with tableside cooking it's important to understand the connection between cooking actions and the finished product, just like in the kitchen.

IT'S NOT JUST SEASONING that is difficult to do in the dining room. How do you thicken a cream sauce in the sauté pan when there really isn't enough time to reduce it? The trick is either to reduce the cream ahead of time or lace it with a slurry of arrowroot—the cream behaves as normal during the preparation, until the pan gets hot enough for the arrowroot to work. Other thickeners, such as potato starch, will also work, just not as quickly. Whichever one is used, be careful with the amount; it should produce the ideal consistency every time.

TABLESIDE COOKING TIPS

- Never, ever touch any of the food with your fingers. (Touching a banana's peel is fine, however.)

- During most tableside cooking, hold the fork in your left hand, spoon in your right. Spoon and fork are held in the same hand only for serving.

- Put the mise en place on the gueridon in the order in which it will be used. It helps you to stay organized when nerves take over.

- If you need to clean off the spoon while cooking, don't whang it on the side of the sauté pan—just wipe off the bottom of the spoon with the fork.

- When sautéing, preheat the pan before adding food. To avoid splattering the guest with hot fat, large pieces of meat or fish should be laid in the pan *toward* you—the opposite of what you would do in the kitchen.

- When moving the finished product to the plate, be careful not to let any of the food fall from the serviceware.

- If you drop something on the floor, don't acknowledge it—most of the guests will never notice.

- Don't be overly meticulous. You don't have to turn over every banana slice or every shrimp in the pan. Guests get bored, and there's other work to do in the service station.

- Keep dishes relatively simple. Don't go overboard with the number of ingredients or complexity of the method.

CAESAR SALAD

This is one of the most famous salads in the world. It was created by Caesar Cardini when some regular customers came by his restaurant in Tijuana, Mexico, for a late-night snack. The kitchen was closed, and he didn't have a whole lot to work with, but he ended up creating a classic. Anchovy-phobes need not worry; whole anchovies are optional as a garnish, and the anchovy in the salad is pounded to a fare-thee-well—out of sight, but necessary for the authentic flavor and balance of the salad.

EQUIPMENT

Gueridon or work surface

Large wooden salad bowl, unfinished

Service spoon and fork

Pepper grinder filled with black peppercorns

Two chilled salad plates

INGREDIENTS

1 clove of garlic, peeled

1 anchovy filet

1 T Dijon mustard

1 pasteurized egg yolk

1/2 lemon, seeds removed

4 oz extra-virgin olive oil, in gooseneck

1 head romaine lettuce, washed and dried, torn into bite-size pieces, rolled in clean cloth napkin

4 T grated Parmigiano Reggiano

3/4 c croutons

METHOD

1. Place garlic clove in bowl. Break up the clove into small pieces with the fork. When pieces are small enough, crush them with the back of the spoon to create a paste. Rub the garlic paste into the wooden bowl, leaving no visible pieces of garlic. Hint: while crushing and rubbing the garlic, hold the bowl with the free fingers of your left (fork) hand.

2. Repeat step 1 with the anchovy filet. Again, when finished there should be no visible sign of the garlic or anchovy.

3. Add mustard to the bowl and distribute evenly over the bottom of the bowl.

4. Add egg yolk, whisking lightly to combine with mustard and to incorporate flavor from garlic and anchovy.

5. Take the lemon half and stick the fork into the cut side, just below the center, with the spoon held just below the fork. The fork will catch any pits that the prep cooks missed, while the juice drips into the spoon. Add the lemon juice to the bowl. Whisk it into the egg-mustard mixture with the fork.

6. Drizzle the olive oil in a circle around the side of the bowl, about halfway down from the edge. This allows the oil to pick up the anchovy and garlic flavor that was rubbed in. Whisk in the oil, creating the finished dressing. It should be slightly thick, with a pleasant yellow color, and should be heady with the aromas of garlic, anchovy, mustard, and lemon.

7. Add the lettuce to the bowl, along with half of the grated cheese. Toss the salad lightly to coat with the dressing and cheese.

8. Ask the guests if they would like some ground black pepper, and comply with their wishes. Add the croutons and toss again to combine.

9. Divide the salad between two chilled salad plates and garnish with the remaining grated cheese.

Yield: 2 servings

STEAK DIANE

As with many other classic dishes, the origins of this dish are shrouded in the past. One story is that it was created for a member of the Vanderbilt family on her private train; another is that it's named after Diana, the Roman goddess of the hunt and the moon.

EQUIPMENT
Gueridon with rechaud
Copper sauté pan
Ramekins for mise en place
Service spoon and fork
2 heated dinner plates

INGREDIENTS
Salt and pepper to taste

2 3-oz beef tenderloin medallions, pounded to $3/8$ inch thick

2 oz olive oil in gooseneck

1 oz whole butter, in pieces

2 T shallots, finely minced

1 T lemon juice

1 t Worcestershire sauce

4 oz demiglace

1 T Dijon mustard

1 oz Armagnac or Cognac

2 oz heavy cream

1 T parsley, chopped

METHOD

1. Light the rechaud and start preheating the pan.

2. Sprinkle salt and grind black pepper onto both sides of each medallion.

3. Put some olive oil in the pan and add a little whole butter. Remember, don't put too much fat in the pan—it's hard to remove it later before making the sauce.

4. When the pan is almost smoking, lay the meat into the pan toward yourself to avoid splattering the guests with hot fat.

5. If there are hot spots in the pan, move the steaks around the pan to achieve even browning. Once the first side is well browned, turn the steaks over.

6. While the steaks brown on the other side, add the shallots to the coolest area of the pan and stir them around until fragrant and translucent.

7. When the steaks are brown but still a bit undercooked, remove them from the pan and place on one of the warmed dinner plates. Invert the other plate over the steaks to keep them warm as you prepare the sauce.

8. Lower the heat to medium, then add the lemon juice and Worcestershire sauce to the pan. Scrape up the browned bits from the pan and let them dissolve into the sauce.

9. Add the demiglace to the pan and whisk in the mustard with the fork.

10. Pour in enough cream to enrich the sauce without lessening its intensity. Allow it to reduce until just before nappé, then return the steaks and their juices to the sauté pan.

11. When the steaks have been coated in and warmed by the sauce, move them to the plate that covered them, and spoon sauce over the top. Potatoes and vegetables should be brought warm from the kitchen on a side dish.

Yield: 1 serving (Note: The dish can be prepared for two if the steaks are cut thicker, the searing temperature is lowered, and the sauce ingredients are doubled.)

BANANAS FOSTER

This dish was invented at Brennan's Restaurant in New Orleans in the 1950s, the result of Owen Brennan's request that the chef come up with a banana recipe for the breakfast menu. At the time, New Orleans was the major port of entry in the United States for bananas from South America, and Brennan wanted to showcase the fruit. It's been said that Brennan's goes through thirty-five thousand pounds of bananas annually, just for this dish. It is simple to prepare and absolutely delicious. The bananas can come out of the kitchen already cut into slices, or you can use the method below, which is not difficult and is pretty darned impressive to the guest.

EQUIPMENT

Gueridon with rechaud
Copper sauté pan
Ramekins for mise en place
Service spoon and fork
Utility knife or sharp dinner knife
Bottles of liqueur (crème de banane and dark rum) with pour spouts

INGREDIENTS

2 oz whole butter, chilled, cut into pieces
2 oz brown sugar
2 bananas, whole, in peel
1 oz crème de banane
1 oz dark rum (Myers's or something similar)
Cinnamon in a shaker to taste
2 bowls vanilla ice cream

METHOD

1. Light the rechaud and set on a low flame. Put all of the butter and sugar in the pan and set it over the flame so that the ingredients will start melting while you prepare the bananas.

2. Cut banana peel at the base of the stem. Make two longitudinal cuts in the peel from the cut at the stem down to the base, approximately 1 inch apart. Switch from knife to fork and slip a tine of the fork under one segment of the peel, close to the stem cut. Roll one segment of banana peel off toward yourself (like opening a sardine can), leaving the rest of the peel in place.

3. Pick up the knife again and cut the banana into slices, from stem to bottom, while still inside the banana skin. The last cut should be right above that little nub at the bottom. The very end of the banana has some tannic taste to it and should be left behind during step number seven.

4. Repeat the above steps with the second banana.

5. While preparing the bananas for cooking, you should have been keeping an eye on the sauce to make sure that it didn't burn. Now raise the heat of the rechaud, and combine the melted butter with the sugar using the spoon and fork.

6. Remove the pan from the heat, add the crème de banane, return the pan to the rechaud, and stir until the sauce is smooth.

7. When the sauce has come together, add the bananas to the pan. Hold each banana close to the pan and parallel to it—you want to avoid splashing yourself or a guest with the hot sauce. Use the spoon to lift the upper edge of the banana peel away from the slices and gently pull at the slices with the service spoon. The slices should fall easily out of the banana peel and into the pan.

8. Stir the banana slices with some vigor so that they will be covered in sauce and heated on both sides. It is too time-consuming to flip each banana piece individually, so just turn over the ones that seem a bit raw on top. When the edges of the banana slices begin to look a little rounded, they are probably heated through. Very ripe bananas are more yielding, so be careful not to turn them into mush.

9. With the spoon, move the banana slices and most of the sauce to the half of the pan closest to you to make a clear space for the flambé. Place that area of the pan above the flame. For the rum to flame, it has to be vaporized by contact with a hot pan—the alcohol vapor is what ignites.

10. When the cleared part of the pan begins to smoke a bit or shows some signs of browning, pull the pan off the flame, add the rum to it, and roll the alcohol toward the front of the pan. As it flames up, put down the rum bottle and pick up the cinnamon shaker. Before the flames die down, add two shakes of cinnamon to the pan through the flame. The cinnamon adds a nice flavor, and also sparkles like fireworks as it passes through the flame, sending a lovely aroma through the dining room.

11. Stir to combine the flamed rum and cinnamon, then serve over vanilla ice cream.

Yield: 2 servings

CAFFÈ STANZIONE

This flaming coffee is a great way to introduce your staff to open flames in the dining room, and it's also a crowd-pleaser, both because of the entertainment value and because it's delicious. The three liqueurs used can be mixed and matched, for instance, depending on the cuisine of the restaurant. There are, though some rules. The first and last liqueurs are flamed, so they should be around 80 proof (which is 40 percent alcohol). The proof level of the middle liqueur doesn't matter. In fact, the middle ingredient doesn't have to have any alcohol whatsoever, and it could be a flavored syrup such as the ones used in coffee shops. Mix and match—experiment with different ingredients to create a signature coffee drink for your restaurant. (Note: To use this method, it has to be prepared two at a time because of the initial flaming style, which was originally developed by legendary mixologist "Professor" Jerry Thomas at the El Dorado Bar in San Francisco for his Blue Blazer Cocktail.)

EQUIPMENT

Gueridon

Two stemmed glasses

Two heat sources (Sterno works fine)

Liqueur bottles

Silver coffee server

Container for whipped cream

Metal ladle with pouring lip

Two cloth napkins, ready to be tied around the glasses

Two small plates lined with doilies

INGREDIENTS

1½ oz brandy

10–12 oz strong black coffee (decaffeinated if requested)

2 oz dark crème de cacao

³/₄ c whipped cream, unsweetened

2 oz orange liqueur, such as Gran Gala or Grand Marnier

METHOD

1. Light heat sources.

2. Hold glasses by stem, with pinkies under the base for stability. Tilt glasses over the two flames and rotate them slowly above the flames. The idea here is to heat the glasses enough that the brandy will flame. Rotating the glasses keeps them from being shattered from the direct heat of the flame.

3. When the glasses are heated, place them on the gueridon and add half the brandy to each glass. Pick up the glasses and tilt them toward the flames. The flames will jump into the glasses.

4. Pour the flaming brandy from glass to glass five or six times. This is for show, but if the guests ask why you do this, tell them that it's to warm the glasses to keep the coffee from getting cold.

5. Put down the glasses again and add half the coffee to each glass. This will put out any flames that are still burning. Leave about 1½ inches of space at the top of the glass.

6. Add half the dark crème de cacao to each glass.

7. Add the whipped cream to the top of each drink—you want it to float on top.

8. Heat the metal ladle over one of the flames. Add all the orange liqueur to the ladle and hold it over the heat source until it flames.

9. Ladle half the flaming liqueur into each of the coffee glasses. Start with the ladle close to the glass, then raise the ladle as you pour, creating a stream of blue fire going into the glass. The more confident you get, the higher you can go.

10. Wrap or tie the napkins around the glasses, place them on the doily-covered plates, and serve.

Yield: 2 servings

Why bother with such elaborate preparations? Isn't this all a little old-school? To a certain degree, yes—but in a good way. Changing some ingredients around or using some modern equipment can easily modernize tableside preparation. It is up to you and the chef to come up with new ways to cook in the dining room. Tableside ice cream made in a bowl that's embedded in dry ice? Heck, give it a shot. Guests love it, they'll pay for it, and the staff might just have some fun doing it.

ADDING A FLAMMABLE SUBSTANCE (such as liqueur) to a sauté pan that is right above an open flame can be very dangerous. If the stream of alcohol coming from the bottle is too close to the burner's flame, the fire can travel up that stream and into the bottle, causing the contents to explode and sending flaming alcohol and broken glass all over the guests and your staff. Such a tragedy can be avoided by removing the pan from the rechaud before adding the liqueur. Another method that is used to add liqueur at the point of flambéing is to pull the pan halfway off the rechaud, add the liqueur to the back of the pan, then tilt it forward so the alcohol rushes to the front of the pan, where it ignites; this method is best suited for more experienced servers.

CHAPTER 7:
BEVERAGE
SERVICE

In the very first chapter of this book I introduced the concept of hospitality by comparing what we in the restaurant industry do for our guests to what you do when you're entertaining guests at home. And all across the world, from ancient times until the present moment, one of the very first things you offer a guest in your home is a drink—cool water, carefully prepared tea, a glass of wine, a cocktail. This chapter will discuss the role beverage service plays in welcoming guests to your establishment, and how to run this end of your business smoothly and profitably.

WATER, WATER EVERYWHERE

AS NOTED IN CHAPTER 5, the first sale after a tableful of guests is seated is often bottled water. Sometimes, in fact, waiters can make it seem as if bottled water is practically the only choice, asking, "Sparkling or still . . . or would you just like some tap water?" The waiter, of course, wants to make a sale, but it can be done without making the guest feel like a cheapskate for not spending the money on a bottled variety.

Asking "Would you care for ice water or bottled water?" is, I have found, more hospitable, in that the free option is being offered first, but the potential sale of bottled water is still there. I have observed that bottled water sales do not suffer terribly by using this line at the tables—people who want bottled water will buy it anyway.

Even if bottled water is pushed more heavily, one practice that definitely should be avoided is having the waiter continue to bring bottles of water without asking the guest if more is desired. Think about it this way: would a waiter just keep bringing hamburgers to the table as guests finish theirs? Maybe if Wimpy was at the table, but not in any other circumstance.

If guests are concerned about the quality of the local water, it's smart to install a water filtration system. Most commercial ice-making machines require them anyway, so a somewhat larger filtration system allows the waiter to offer filtered ice water.

COCKTAIL HOUR?

UP UNTIL THE EARLY 1990S, most guests would have a cocktail, or maybe two, before even looking at the dinner menu. Of course, many Americans continued to drink cocktails through the rest of the meal, because wine wasn't big yet. As wine became more popular, it nudged cocktails out of the scene for a little while.

However, there has been a resurgence of interest in cocktails of late, partly fueled by the popularity of the Cosmopolitan and its starring role on *Sex and the City*. Cocktail menus have been popping up all over the place, perhaps led by the menu created at New York's Rainbow Room by the mixologist Dale "King Cocktail" DeGroff. While this book is not a bartending guide, there is some information that all waiters and dining room staff should know in order to serve guests' needs more efficiently. The introduction of a full bar or cocktail program into a restaurant requires a fair amount of work, but it's worth it. The increased guest satisfaction (as well as beverage sales) usually justifies the investment. That investment is made up of planning, training, and the purchase of equipment and ingredients with which to make the drinks.

To best serve the guest, a waiter needs to know preparation terminology and the names (and basic ingredients) of the most popular cocktails at that restaurant. Going up to the next level of expertise, the staff should know the names of the best-selling spirit brands and have some basic knowledge of those spirits.

COCKTAIL TERMS

- **NEAT.** Something served neat is poured right from the bottle into the glass and presented at room temperature, with nothing added to it. Some spirits that might be served this way are many whiskeys (usually in a rocks or old-fashioned glass), and anything that is an unmixed shot drink. Beverages served this way are appropriately served in a liqueur or pony glass.

- **UP, STRAIGHT UP.** The spirit or mixed drink is served chilled, without ice. Some cocktails are traditionally served up (the Cosmopolitan), while with others it is an alternative to the drink being served on the rocks (Martinis and Manhattans). Chill the drink by stirring it with ice cubes and then strain the drink into a stemmed glass, leaving the ice behind.

- **ROCKS.** A drink ordered on the rocks is served over ice, usually in an Old-Fashioned glass, sometimes referred to as a rocks glass. The ice is usually placed in the glass first, and then the spirit or drink poured over it. This includes mixed drinks that have been made in a shaker—it is classy to strain the cocktail into a rocks glass that has fresh ice cubes in it, rather than use the partially melted ice that the drink was shaken with.

- **TALL, SHORT.** For cocktails using a spirit plus a mixer, a tall drink is served in a highball glass, sometimes referred to as a Collins glass. A short drink is served in a rocks glass. In either case, the pour (portion) of liquor is the same—the difference is the amount of mixer that joins the spirit in the glass. With drinks such as Gin and Tonic, the default is to serve it tall; this is supposed to be a refreshing drink, and a healthy amount of tonic water will guarantee that. Some Scotch drinkers, however, prefer their Scotch and Water on the short side, with less dilution from the mixer, and in fact the tall/short terminology is most often used by whiskey drinkers.

From left to right: grappa glass, Martini glass, Manhattan, pony/sherry glass, highball/Collins glass, rocks/old-fashioned glass, brandy snifter, glass for single-malt Scotch, pilsner glass

SHAKEN OR STIRRED?

SHAKING AERATES AND MIXES DRINKS, often making them taste better—that's why we shake drinks made with fruit juices, as well as cream drinks. Why, then, is it incorrect to shake other drinks? Part of the enjoyment of many alcohol-only cocktails (such as a Martini) is the crystal-clear quality of the liquor, and shaking such a drink introduces thousands of tiny bubbles that disrupt that clarity. Second, it is important to keep dilution to a minimum during the preparation of a drink that is made mainly from liquor. Stirring a drink such as a Manhattan or Rob Roy with good-sized ice cubes will chill the drink (giving it a noticeable viscosity, which contributes to mouth feel) without introducing too much water, as shaking could do.

"Ice cubes" means *cubes*, not slivers or mini-cubes or mini ice doughnuts. The quality and size of the ice cubes used can make a huge difference in the final quality of the drinks that the bartender can produce. A good-sized ice cube (1¼ to 1½ inches) allows the bartender to make better drinks. If the drink is shaken or stirred, the lower surface area of the larger cubes will allow the drink to be chilled with less dilution. For rocks or highball drinks, the larger cubes will last longer, keeping a Scotch on the Rocks from turning rapidly into a Scotch and Water.

SPIRITS 101

Here is a brief primer on the most popular spirits used in restaurants these days. This is not, in any way, a definitive guide to alcoholic potables—it is merely intended to convey some information that will foster clear communication between guests and staff.

VODKA

This is the most popular distilled spirit in the United States today. Its flavor and aroma are purposely not distinctive in the same way those of other liquors are, but the many varieties of vodka offer subtle distinctions. Vodka distilled from grain is considered superior because of its clean flavor, while potato vodkas are prized for their smooth body.

FLAVORED VODKAS ARE BIG THESE DAYS. Lemon, raspberry, and even vanilla and chocolate are available now. They are often used in cocktails (the Cosmopolitan), but I think that they are at their best either on the rocks or with club soda.

Popular brands include Absolut, Finlandia, Stolichnaya, and Smirnoff. Luxury brands include Ketel One, Belvedere, Chopin, Hangar One, Grey Goose, and Tanqueray Sterling.

Cocktails made with vodka include Vodka Martini, Screwdriver, Bloody Mary, Salty Dog, Gimlet, Greyhound, Cape Codder, Bay Breeze, Sea Breeze, and Madras.

GIN

This grain-based spirit is flavored with juniper berries. *London dry gin* is relatively light and crisp and is ideal for Martini and other cocktail recipes. *American dry gin* is of a somewhat less impressive pedigree, although there are some perfectly sound examples. It is at its best when mixed. *Holland* or *genever gin* has more flavor and body than London dry gin and is more often imbibed chilled and straight.

Popular brands include Beefeater, Bombay, Boodles, Gilbey's, Gordon's, Seagram's, and Tanqueray. Luxury brands include Bombay Sapphire, Tanqueray Ten, and Van Gogh. Cocktails made with gin include Martini, Bronx, Gimlet, Gin and Tonic, Gin and It, Negroni, Gibson, Singapore Sling, Fitzgerald, and Tom Collins.

RUM

Rum is a distillate of sugarcane, sugar beets, molasses, or other sugar by-products. Puerto Rico is the largest producer. Color in rum comes in part from the type of container it is aged in, but in addition many rums have caramel coloring added. *Light rums* have a little molasses flavor, though some approach the neutrality of vodka. *Amber rum* is a bit darker and more flavorful. *Añejo* (which means "aged") is usually a premium bottling by a rum producer and is smoother and more complex. *Dark rum*, fermented longer before distillation, is the most aromatic, with a richer flavor.

Popular brands include Appleton, Bacardi, Gosling's, Mount Gay, Myers's, and Ron Rico. Cocktails made with rum include Bacardi Cocktail, Cuba Libre, Daiquiri, Planter's punch, Piña Colada, Rum and Tonic, Mai Tai, and Jamaican Rum Punch.

TEQUILA

There has been a surge in the popularity of this spirit over the last ten years, mostly because of the appeal of the Margarita and this spirit's newfound fame as a shot drink. Though you might associate shots with a bar rather than a restaurant, high-quality tequila (which, by the way, comes only from the area of Tequila in the Mexican state of Jalisco; the same spirit from other parts of the country is called *mezcal*) is a fine spirit that is sometimes served in a shot glass as a sipping spirit. All tequila is produced from the agave plant, with blue agave often considered the best type; some premium bottles are labeled "100 percent blue agave." *Silver* or *plata tequila* is not aged and is usually the best choice for mixing; *reposado* is aged for at least one year in oak; *añejo* is aged for at least two. Aged tequilas tend to be smoother than the unaged ones and are most often the ones served neat.

Popular brands include Jose Cuervo, Sauza, Porfidio, Patrón, Monte Alban (mezcal), and Herradura. Cocktails made with tequila include Margarita and Tequila Sunrise.

WHISKEY

Whiskeys are produced from a grain mash that has been fermented, distilled, and then aged in a wood barrel. It is the barrel aging that gives whiskeys their color and characteristic flavor, which differentiate them from clear grain spirits. The distinctions between whiskeys result from the base grain used and the production methods, including aging.

The most famous type of American whiskey is *bourbon*. Made predominantly from corn, with wheat and barley sometimes included, it tends to be full-bodied and round, with a slight nutty sweetness. Popular brands include Wild Turkey, Jim Beam, Heaven Hill, Maker's Mark, Old Grand-Dad, I. W. Harper, and Evan Williams. Premium, single-barrel, and small-batch bourbons include Basil Hayden's, Knob Creek, Booker's, Baker's (all made by Jim Beam), Blanton's, and Pappy Van Winkle. Cocktails made with bourbon include the Bourbon Manhattan and Bourbon Sour, but most are consumed neat, on the rocks, or with water or soda.

Canadian whiskey is generally of high quality; the use of rye as one of the grains from which it is distilled gives this light-bodied, distinctively flavored whiskey its nickname, *rye whiskey.* Because of its relative delicacy, it is very popular for mixed drinks and cocktails. Popular brands include Black Velvet, Canadian Club, Seagram's 7, Seagram's VO, Seagram's Crown Royal, and Schenley O.F.C. Cocktails made with it include Manhattan, Dry Manhattan, Perfect Manhattan, Whiskey Sour, 7 and 7, and Old- Fashioned.

Irish whiskey can be made from barley, corn, rye, oats, and wheat, although barley usually predominates. It is on the light and delicate side of the whiskey spectrum, and it is usually served neat or on the rocks. Popular brands include Bushmills, Jameson's, John Powers, Tullamore Dew, and Murphy's. The only mixed drink usually made with Irish whiskey is Irish Coffee.

Scotch whiskey has a distinctive smoky flavor that derives from the use of peat-fueled fires to dry the grain during the production process. Because of that smokiness, Scotch tends to be more of an acquired taste than the others and isn't as adaptable to cocktail recipes as, say, bourbon and Canadian whiskeys. *Single-malt Scotch whiskey* is the product of a single distillery (there are hundreds of distilleries in Scotland), with differences in flavor coming from the grain and water used, and even from the type of peat. Regional commonalities can help you to group the whiskeys by flavor characteristics. The regions are the Highlands (with four subregions), Campbeltown, Speyside, Islay (pronounced "EYE-luh"), and the Lowlands. *Blended Scotch whiskeys* are available at many price points and quality levels, their strongest suit being consistency and relative simplicity compared to the single-malt whiskeys. Popular single-malt Scotches include Macallan, Oban, Glenfiddich, Glenlivet, Laphroaig, and Knockando. Popular blended Scotches include Dewar's White Label, Johnnie Walker, Chivas Regal, Pinch, Cutty Sark, J&B (Justerini & Brooks),

HERE'S A TIP THAT I LEARNED WHILE BARTENDING—Scotch drinkers don't like it when you throw away the ice from their first drink while preparing their second. They say that the ice is "marinated" or "broken in." What's really happening here is that the melted ice in the bottom of the glass dilutes the newly added whiskey and makes it ready to drink sooner.

Passport, Teacher's, Ballantine, and John Begg. Cocktails made with Scotch whiskey include Scotch on the Rocks, Scotch and Water, Scotch and Soda, Scotch Sour, Blood and Sand, and Rob Roy.

BEER

BEER IS MADE USING A FEW BASIC INGREDIENTS: malted grain (barley, wheat, or rye; the degree to which the malt is roasted affects the flavors and color of the finished beer), water (the quality of water can be significant), yeast (of which there are many different strains), and hops (bitter-tasting flowers that both balance the rich, sweet flavor of the malt and add to the shelf life of the beer).

The finished product falls into one of two categories. The most popular beers in this country are *lagers*, such as Budweiser, Miller Genuine Draft, and Coors. Fermented at cooler temperatures (bottom-fermented), they have a crisp, clean taste. The most popular types of lager include pilsner and bock. *Ales*, fermented at higher temperatures (top-fermented), are more complex, with a fruitier taste and aroma. Types of ale include India pale ale, stout, porter, and lambic.

SERVING AND STORING BEER

As a rule of thumb, the more complex the flavors of the beer, the higher the serving temperature should be. Most Americans, of course, prefer their beer ice cold, but most beers, even lagers, could stand to be served a little bit warmer. Suggested serving temperatures are as follows:

- Pale lagers: 45–50°F

- Pale ales/dark lagers: 50°55°F

- Dark ales: 55–60°F

A general rule is the higher the alcohol content, the higher the serving temperature. However, storage temperature is another issue—too high a temperature risks shortening the beverage's life span, and too low a temperature induces cloudiness. Beers should be stored upright in a cool, dark place, as sunlight causes deterioration and what is often referred to as a "skunky" aroma; even diffuse daylight and normal fluorescent light can cause quality loss. Avoid agitating beer, as that will hasten oxidation.

IT'S PRETTY EASY to get dark beers to a proper serving temperature. First, the refrigerator they're served from can be adjusted to a slightly higher temperature, such as 45° F. Then pour the beer into a room-temperature glass rather than a frozen mug, and you're just about there.

ALES HAVE BEEN AROUND FOR MANY YEARS (three-thousand-year-old beer vessels have been found in Israel) and tend to have a bit more flavor than their lager counterparts, mostly because of the warmer fermentation, which creates more complex flavors. Their styles range from bitter with hops to rich with malt, and they can range in color from blond to almost black. With such a range available, the common thread is that they tend to have more complexity than lagers, and should be served at a warmer temperature than most Americans would think.

GLASSWARE FOR BEER

The glassware used to serve beer will depend upon the type the guest has ordered. Pilsner glasses are appropriate for most lagers, but fine ales should be served in more of a goblet because of their more complex aroma. The omnipresent pilsner glass does dominate the bar scene across America, but the increasing popularity of Belgian and Belgian-style beer is bringing with it a consciousness of what glass a beer should be served in. In fact, certain brewers such as Chimay (Belgium) and Ommegang (Cooperstown, New York) have pouring instructions and glassware recommendations right on the label.

BEER-FOOD PAIRINGS

Pizza, burgers, and barbecue are all classic food matches for beer, but it doesn't have to stop there. Germany, Belgium, and Alsace in France, all traditional producers of quality beers, have cuisines that also embrace the beverage. The most important technical aspect of matching beer to food involves taking into account the fact that most beer doesn't have an acid component to counteract the richness of food. The bitterness supplied by hops, however, can help to cut the cloying effect of richness in food. Try out some combinations, and you won't write beer off as a serious accompaniment to good food.

WINE

WINE IS THE CLASSIC ACCOMPANIMENT to good food. A carefully selected wine enhances the guest's dining experience, and I believe deeply that it's our job to make it easier for our guests to order wine. And the guest isn't the only one who benefits—the easier it is for guests to order a bottle, the more of it you'll sell.

To learn everything about wine is virtually impossible—even if you memorize every grape, town, winery, and wine law (which would be near impossible), every year there is a new vintage of every wine. Below you will find some basic but fundamental information, as well as a conceptual approach to selecting a wine.

GRAPES

It all starts with the grape. There's a saying in the wine business: "God gives us the grapes—try not to mess it up." Wine is an agricultural product. The grape crop depends on the weather and many environmental conditions to flourish. Interestingly, grapes grown in relatively poor conditions often show more character. The best grape for wine is one that has a balance between sugar and acidity, so the finished wine will have both fruity flavor and tartness. The most important grapes in the restaurant business today are as follows:

WHITE-WINE GRAPES

- **CHARDONNAY.** In New World growing regions this grape produces a rich wine that is usually aged in oak barrels to add complexity and body.

- **SAUVIGNON BLANC.** Often thought of as the main alternative to Chardonnay because it is so different, it usually has an herbal or "green" quality that is a contrast to the rich, buttery flavor of oaked Chardonnays.

- **RIESLING.** While the least popular of the three, it has the best potential to go with a broad range of food. People thrown off by sweetness can get bone-dry Rieslings from Alsace, France.

RED-WINE GRAPES

- **MERLOT.** The most popular red grape right now, it yields relatively soft, warm wines with relatively low acid levels. This leads to a wine that tastes good by itself but often lacks the acidity needed to go with food.

DID YOU KNOW THAT White Zinfandel comes from a red grape? In fact, most high-quality rosé wines are made from red grapes. The thing is, almost all grape juice is white in color; the red color comes from allowing the juice of the crushed grapes to remain in contact with the grape skins. So if they crush the grapes and leave the skins in for only a little while . . . you guessed it: pink wine.

- **CABERNET SAUVIGNON.** Wines from this grape usually have more structure, acidity, and aging potential. With flavors of black currant and green bell pepper, and sometimes with daunting tannins, it can often use a little softening up by adding Merlot—and this is exactly what they do in Bordeaux.

- **PINOT NOIR.** I have to admit a personal fondness for this grape. It produces wines that have the same flavor intensity as most food—not like Cabernet, which can overpower food. Pinot Noir is known for its profuse aromas and its earthiness. That and its good level of acidity make it one of the most flexible food wines.

- **SYRAH/SHIRAZ.** This grape is becoming quite popular in the United States, mostly because of Australian imports. It's got obvious berry flavors and often a distinctly spicy character—to the point where you can actually smell white pepper sometimes. The finest wines made from this grape come from the northern Rhône region of France.

- **ZINFANDEL.** Perhaps known mostly for its so-called white version, Zinfandel is a uniquely American grape that only recently has been linked genetically to the Primitivo grape of Italy. Wines made from this grape are also distinctly American—bold, brawny, and fun. Lots of fruit and spice make it a great wine for American food as well.

THE FLAVORS

The basic terms used to describe the flavors of wine include *fruit, tartness, tannins, body,* and *balance.*

- **FRUIT.** When most people say a wine is fruity, they usually mean it's sweet. Fruit flavors in wine can actually mimic sweetness, so a technically dry wine (one with no residual sugar) can taste sweet. Grapes themselves have a broad range of esters (flavor molecules) that can mimic other fruits. Add to this the fact that fermentation creates other flavors, and you can wind up with aromas of green pepper or strawberry. Remember, most of what we think is taste happens in the nose—so smells turn into flavors.

- **TARTNESS.** Grapes have acid that you can taste and feel (when your mouth waters). The prevalent acid in grapes is malic acid, which is also found in apples. This tartness helps to balance the richness (fat) in food. It's one of the main reasons that we drink wine with food. Think about a great vinaigrette—there's a balance between the oil and vinegar. That's what we're doing when we put wine with food. Acid also happens to be a preservative in wine (remember how lemon juice keeps fruit from turning brown, which is oxidation).

- **TANNINS.** Tannins are a group of highly complex phenolic compounds found in a variety of plants, including grapes. They occur in pits and stems, but mostly in the skins of red grapes. Originally used to tan (waterproof and preserve) leather, they act as a preservative in wine, as well as adding a bitterness and mouth feel that can help add balance to a wine. The mouth feel is a sensation of astringency, like the feeling you get when drinking strong black tea. Tannins usually soften as a wine ages, which is a major part of deciding when a wine is ready to drink.

- **BODY.** The way that wine feels in your mouth (its body) is related to the amount of alcohol in the wine. Alcohol adds body to wine because of glycol,

WHEN I FIRST STARTED LEARNING ABOUT WINE, I thought that the people talking about "red berries" and "black pepper" aromas in wine were making it up. At first, wine just smells like wine. With experience, though, you can start picking up specific smells. The first one that I ever got was the aroma of violets in a Clos de Vougeot (red Burgundy). To this day, it's still my favorite red wine.

MALOLACTIC FERMENTATION OCCURS when bacteria get into the wine and convert malic (apple) acid into lactic (milk) acid. Lactic acid is less strong than malic, so a wine that has undergone malolactic fermentation feels softer and tastes less sour. Almost all red wines go through this process, and some whites. Most notably, big oaky California Chardonnays that go through "malo" have a richer aspect because of it.

the alcohol-related sugar. More alcohol means fuller body. To discern the body of a wine you're drinking, think about dairy products for a minute. Skim milk is light-bodied; cream is full-bodied. Apply the same idea to the wine in your mouth. Body can be important when matching wine with food—big wine (Napa Valley Cabernet) overpowers light food (boneless chicken breast), and light wine (Muscadet) tastes watery with big food (grilled salmon).

- **BALANCE.** One of the true signs of quality in a wine is that all of the flavors mentioned above are in balance. A wine that is neither too fruity nor too tart, with a nice complexity of flavor, gives you a well-rounded drinking experience. It's also one of the hardest things for a winemaker to achieve.

HOW TO THINK ABOUT WINE: THE QUADRANT SYSTEM

There are many books about wine—and most of them just add to the confusion. The amount of knowledge required to be a wine expert is staggering, and impossible to bestow upon every member of the floor staff. Thus, you need to simplify it for the people you're training. To me, this means going conceptual rather than informational. You can get your staff to think about wine in a way that will aid in getting wine on the table.

Since wine is about flavor, it helps to know what flavors are going to be in a bottle without even opening it. If you know what grape it is and where the wine is from, it's fair to say that you'll be able to predict the basic flavors of it. Conversely, if you know what the guest wants (dry and full-bodied), you know where to look for that style. Here's how.

NORTH OR SOUTH?

The body of the wine depends largely on where it's from—more precisely, the climate it's from. Colder regions tend to produce light-bodied, high-acid wines because the grapes don't get as ripe. Warmer regions usually put out fuller wines with a bit less acidity. So if a party of guests wants a full-bodied wine because of the food they chose, look to warmer areas such as southern France (the Rhône or Provence) or the Napa Valley. For lighter-bodied, check out the Alto Adige of Italy or Oregon.

OLD WORLD OR NEW WORLD?

There is a basic difference between the wines of Europe and those of the United States, South America, and Australia. It comes down to this: in the Old World wine is an accompaniment to food, and in the New World it's a beverage. That is, Old World wines tend to be earthier, drier, and missing some fruit, which helps them to accent

GROWS TOGETHER, GOES TOGETHER

ONE METHOD OF MATCHING WINE TO FOOD is to go local. Especially in the Old World, certain grapes have grown alongside other agricultural products for hundreds of years. Through natural and human selection, we have food and wine that are almost literally made for each other. So if the dish you're matching wine to has provenance, go local with the wine—for an Alsatian dish such as Choucroute Garni, try an Alsatian Gewürztraminer; with a Provençal Lamb Stew, a little Bandol Rouge would be fantastic.

food. New World wines, often drunk by themselves, need to be a complete flavor.

The lack of fruity sweetness in European wines is exactly why they go well with food—the food and wine together make a complete flavor experience. New World wines can sometimes clash with food because the wine has all the flavor it needs.

Put these two axes together and place them on a map. You will now be able to find a light-bodied fruity wine by looking for a cold region in the New World, such as Washington state. Does the guest need a full, dry red wine to go with a big steak? Try southern Italy, perhaps the Campania region. Instead of memorizing thousands of facts and names, just look at the map broken into four quadrants. This will make it easier to sell wine and please guests at the same time.

WHAT IF THE GUEST DOESN'T KNOW?

The subject of pairing wine to food is too big to go into detail here, but there are a few simple rules that can be applied at the table.

- If the guest is drinking the wine as a cocktail before dinner, the wine should have some fruit—stick with the New World.

- White with fish, red with meat is somewhat passé these days, because body ends up being more important. With a light dish (such as a ceviche), choose a light wine. Big food (a rib-eye steak) needs big wine.

- Sometimes contrast works well, such as pairing an acidic wine like Sancerre with a rich dish like Scallops in Beurre Blanc. The acidity of the wine cuts through the fat of the dish.

- If a guest comments on a particularly good (or bad) pairing, take a mental note and make that suggested pairing again (or not).

Keep in mind that a table of four people is likely to order all different things, so finely tuned wine pairing goes out the window anyway, unless you only go with wines by the glass. Usually the best answer is to recommend wines that are flexible with a range of foods—the aforementioned Riesling and Pinot Noir come to mind. Also, there is something miraculous about good Chianti with food. By itself it can be uninspiring, but put it on the table with food and all the flavors wake up. So when people order different things, shoot for the middle and you will make everybody happy.

WINE LISTS

When it comes to the wine list, simple is good. Graphics, the font style and size, the number of choices, and the way that the list is organized (by country, for instance) can all have an impact on the customer's ability to make a selection. In a fast-paced, high-volume restaurant, a well-chosen but small wine list can speed the bottle selection process, making it easier for the guest, not to mention the wait staff.

STAFF AND TRAINING

In restaurants where the wine program is more extensive, you owe it to your guests to have a staff that can simplify the wine ordering process. Perhaps best is to have a sommelier—a person who knows the wines on the list and the flavors of the food on the menu (and who is adept at reading guests) can help guests to get what they want while easing the burden of the waiters. Failing that, the wait staff should be trained to sell wine. Tastings, seminars, even external wine courses can be part of a wine training program for the staff. Pre-service meetings should include wine information, perhaps suggested wines to go with the specials, or some basic wine education. The wait staff's knowledge need not go beyond the boundaries of the restaurant's own wine list, but having some basic wine principles under their belts can help the waiters to help the customer.

WINE SERVICE

OPENING WINE

Before opening any bottle of wine, show the bottle to the host or person who ordered it. The guest should have a chance to confirm that it is the correct bottle (including vintage). Always open the bottle within sight of the guests—in a more formal setting this should be done on a flat, stable surface such as a gueridon or side stand. The illustrations on the next two pages demonstrate how to open both still and sparkling wines.

OPENING STILL WINES

1. Present the bottle to the person who ordered it, cradling it in a serviette so the entire label is visible and can be read.

2. Place the bottle on a flat surface and remove the foil covering the cork. Cut around the front of the neck of the bottle just below the second lip.

3. Cut the foil around the back of the neck just below the second lip.

4. Peel away the top of the foil, lifting it away using the blade from the corkscrew and holding the neck of the bottle with the left hand. The server should place the cut foil in his or her pocket.

5. Insert the corkscrew slightly off center at a slight angle and straighten it up with one or two turns. The corkscrew is turned until only one notch of the spiral is left above the cork.

6. Tilt the corkscrew so that the notch in the lever will rest on the lip of the bottle. Hold it in place with the index finger while bracing the neck of the bottle.

7. Pull the corkscrew straight up while continuing to hold the lever in place and brace the neck of the bottle. Be careful not to touch the lip of the bottle.

8. Twist the cork, holding it in a napkin to release it from the bottle opening.

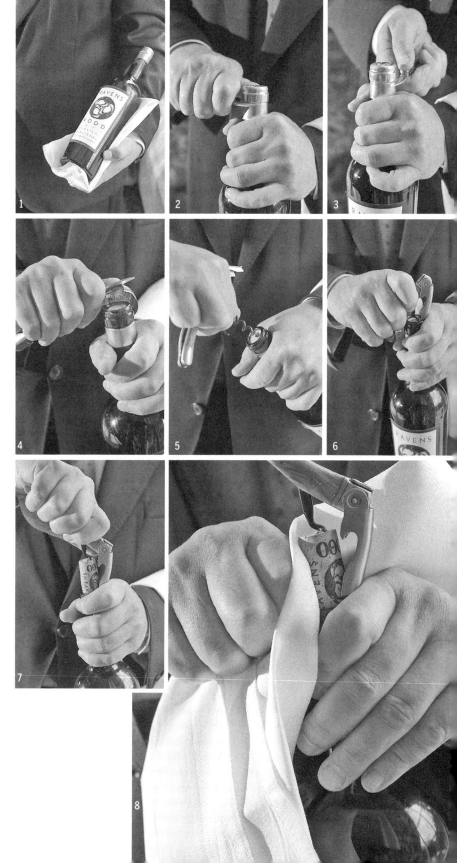

OPENING SPARKLING WINES

1. Present the bottle to the person who ordered it, cradling it in a serviette so the entire label is visible and can be read.

2. Holding the bottle in the serviette, remove the foil from the wire cage.

3. Holding the thumb on top of the cork and applying slight pressure, loosen the wire cage with the other hand.

4. Holding the base of the bottle in one hand, place the napkin over the cork. Hold the cork still while twisting the bottle. As the cork pushes out, hold it tightly. The cork should come out slowly and make a slight "shhh" sound.

5. Gently remove the cork from the bottle.

WINEGLASSES

The glasses must be on the table before the wine is opened. To get the glasses to the table, either carry them upside down between the fingers (see illustration in Chapter 5) or carry them on a tray.

There is a huge variety of wineglasses on the market. Lately the trend has been to use very large ones, some holding as much as 20 fluid ounces, even though the normal portion of wine is 4–5 ounces; the extra room provides space for the aroma of the wine to accumulate, allowing the taster to enjoy the bouquet. This isn't necessary, though—wine can be enjoyed in simple glasses.

From right to left: Champagne glass, white-wine glass, reserve-white glass, red-wine glass, Bordeaux/Tuscany glass, Burgundy/Piedmont glass

Whatever glasses you use, they must be spotless. If the dishwashing machine leaves spots, the rinsing agent should be checked, but the glasses should be steamed and polished anyway (see Chapter 4)—rinsing agents and detergent may leave a residue on the glass that can negatively affect the flavor of the wine.

WINE AT THE TABLE

When the bottle has been opened, pour a 1- to 2-ounce taste of the wine for the host. This allows the guest to return the wine if it is tainted. Once the wine has been approved, pour an appropriate amount for each of the guests, ladies first, finally pouring an equivalent portion for the host (male or female).

Place still wines on a coaster or small plate on the table. White wine can be left on the table or put into an ice bucket, whichever the guest prefers. (In fact, most white wine is served too cold in the United States, and leaving the wine on the table to warm slightly can bring out previously unnoticed complexity of flavor.) Sparkling wine should always be kept in an ice bucket.

In a formal setting, the guest should never have to touch the bottle—the waiters should do all the refilling of glasses. In more casual restaurants, it is acceptable for the guests to pour for themselves.

When a bottle is finished, the waiter should ask the host if another bottle of the same wine should be brought to the table. The host may also prefer to see the wine list again to choose another wine.

ONE PROBLEM THAT HAS ARISEN with the use of extra-large wineglasses is that some guests are disappointed when they see the seemingly meager portion in the bottom of an oversized glass. The explanation that the portion is normal and that the glass just makes it look like less usually goes nowhere. After dealing with more than a handful of unhappy guests, I've decided that it's best to avoid the problem by using smaller glasses for wines sold by the glass, with the larger glasses available upon request.

BAD BOTTLES

The fact is that about one in ten bottles of wine can be considered faulty in one way or another. *Corkiness*, or the wine being "corked," refers to the presence of cork mold or a chemical called trichloroanisole (TCA) in the wine. It results in a musty or moldy smell in the wine and is considered a fault. Other potential faults in wine including *volatile acidity* and *madeirization* (in essence, being "cooked") due to poor storage conditions. This is important to know because the odds are fairly good that a guest who says he or she doesn't like the wine may in fact be reacting to a fault in the wine itself. Ninety-nine times out of a hundred, I will take back a bottle of wine, good or bad, that the guest wants to return. If it's bad, a reputable wine distributor will give you credit for the bottle. If nothing's wrong with the wine, you have a few choices. You can sell the rest of it off by the glass to cover the cost. You can drink it with your own dinner at the end of the night. Or you can do what I do: let the staff taste the wine at the end of the night. You can write it off as a training expense, and you're helping your staff by giving them an opportunity to educate themselves.

RESPONSIBLE BEVERAGE SERVICE

AS RESTAURATEURS, we have a legal and moral obligation to ensure the safety of our guests while they are in our care, and on their trip home insofar as possible. The service of alcoholic beverages brings with it some heady responsibility. We are dispensing a legal drug, and carelessness on our part can result in the death of a guest or someone else on the road. There are many beverage-service training courses out there now, some available from the National Restaurant Association and other industry leaders. Whether your staff is trained through an outside program or in-house, they must be aware of the legal aspects of serving alcohol.

THE LAWS

The legal drinking age in most states is now twenty-one. Guests who want to purchase alcoholic beverages must have proof of age on their person in case it needs to be checked. If there is *any question* whether the guest is of age, I recommend asking for a legal form of identification. In fact, in our restaurant now, we will check the ID of anyone who looks younger than thirty. It really is not worth taking a chance when the well-being of the guest, your staff, and the innocents on the road are all at stake. If a staff member is uncomfortable checking identification, the manager should be the one who does the dirty work. Emotions run strong in this area—the staff should be encouraged to handle the problem on their own, but be there to back them up. There are lots of false IDs on the streets these days, so knowing exactly what the driver's licenses of your state and neighboring states look like is important. You also need to know what constitutes a valid ID for your state.

Anyone who serves alcohol to an obviously intoxicated guest or to a minor is potentially breaking the law. If the person who has been served goes out and hurts himself or herself, or someone else, the server can be held liable for some or all of the injuries in forty-two states and the District of Columbia (though the stringency of these laws varies from state to state). Check with your state's liquor control board to be certain as to your liability.

The legal definition of intoxication in most states is a blood alcohol content (BAC) of .08 percent or higher. To reach a level of .08 percent, a 170-pound male would have to consume approximately four drinks, on an empty stomach, in a one-hour period.

As noted in Chapter 5, the process of telling a guest that he or she cannot have any more alcohol is rarely, if ever, an easy proposition. One thing that doesn't work is the avoidance method—staying away from a table (or guest) that has been cut off. This invariably leads to frustration on the part of the guests, and it can get them agitated even before they know that they will not be served any more alcohol. I have found that a direct approach, with a show of genuine concern for the welfare of the guest, usually works best. I offer such guests any nonalcoholic beverage on the house, as well as discuss with them the fact that I want them to get home safely. Sometimes guests are belligerent and demand more alcohol. They could say that they aren't driving, or that their hotel is right around the corner. None of these assurances is enough. There is always a chance that the guest might somehow end up behind the wheel of a car and hurt someone. The guest who has been cut off might call you names and declare that he or she will never come to your establishment again. My view is that while the guest might not come back to my restaurant, at least he or she will be alive to go to others. Offer to call a cab or find the guest another way to get home. As a last resort, warn the guest that if he or she tries to drive, you will call the police—and then follow through if necessary.

COFFEE AND TEA

COFFEE CAN BE ALMOST A RELIGION. Similarly, tea drinkers can be very particular about how their favorite hot beverage is served. This section will give you some tips about how to please even the coffee or tea connoisseur.

COFFEE

Coffee preparation can be placed into two stylistic categories, American and espresso.

AMERICAN COFFEE

Americans drink a lot of coffee, and they drink it everywhere—diners, specialty cafés, football games, truck stops, diners, PTA meetings. In general, Americans prefer a somewhat less intense, lighter-roast coffee than do Europeans. In restaurants, cups usually have a capacity of 5 to 8 ounces; they should be preheated and placed on the right side of the place setting, with the handle at four o'clock. Make sugar and artificial sweeteners available, and offer cream, half and half, or milk.

While most guests will drink coffee at the end of the meal, some start off with it. Refills should still be offered throughout the meal (at no charge). If the guest has slowed down or stopped, the cup should be removed. Even if not, the guest should be offered a new cup for the coffee to be served after the meal. Timing is important. In formal dining, coffee is considered a separate course, to be served after dessert—that's why chocolates and petit fours exist, to be served during the coffee course. Yet most Americans are unaware of this practice, and want their coffee when they want it. That's why it is best for the server to ask the guest when he or she wishes to have the coffee served—with or after dessert.

ESPRESSO

Europeans tend to drink stronger coffee, in smaller amounts than the American public. Because espresso is quite strong, it is most often made one portion at a time. The beans are almost always dark-roasted, and the coffee is ground very fine. Europeans tend not to put any milk products in their coffee after noon, and especially not after dinner.

An automatic espresso machine, as found in many restaurants, supplies the correct pressure of steam at the proper temperature to produce an espresso with the right flavor, and with what is called crema, the medium-brown foam on top of the coffee. The crema produces an amazing aroma and is responsible in part for the mouth feel of good espresso. As the crema dissipates, the coffee is said to "die" and becomes unservable.

To make a proper espresso, the coffee has to be ground properly and tamped into the receiver (sometimes called the handle) just right. These days, most espresso coffee companies are producing espresso pods that remove the guesswork and are usually neater to work with. While freshly ground beans will always be needed to produce the highest-quality cup of espresso, these pods can give you a more consistent product, with less mess. The choice is yours—perfection requires diligence, and perhaps even a dedicated staff person for the coffee station in order to use freshly ground beans. Or you can have a consistent, high-quality product that almost any of your staff will be able to produce by using the pods.

In serving espresso-style coffee:

- A single espresso should take nineteen to twenty-four seconds to extract.

- Espresso and cappuccino cups should be kept upside down on top of the espresso machine—it's intended to be a cup warmer.

- Keep a clean cloth near the base of the machine to wipe coffee off the bottom of the cup before placing it on the saucer.

- Foamed milk should never exceed 158°F, otherwise it tastes scalded.

- Cappuccino is one-third coffee, one-third steamed milk, and one-third foamed milk. Use whole milk for cappuccino unless otherwise requested.

- Latte is one-third coffee, two-thirds steamed milk.

- Caffè macchiato is an espresso "stained" with a dollop of foamed milk.

TEA

The antioxidant properties of tea (especially green tea) have made it a particularly popular choice today, with the trend toward taking care of our health.

Tea service is one of those things that separate the best from the rest. Old-school loose tea service uses a tea service set that includes a teapot and a hot-water pot on one small tray. The hot water is used to dilute the tea when it is brewed to a color that is a bit too dark for the guest. Good tea service requires a bit of specialized equipment, and also some staff training. Using the correct amount of tea leaves for a certain volume of water is vital to the final quality of the cup of tea.

Do some experimentation to determine the amount of tea appropriate for the volume of water in the pot. Many restaurants are now offering a choice of loose teas, usually including at least one plain black tea (black tea is fully fermented), an oolong (partially fermented), green tea (unfermented), flavored tea, and perhaps a tisane (herbal tea) or two. A typical list might include English Breakfast, Assam, Oolong, Earl Grey (flavored with bergamot), Jasmine Pearl green tea, apple spice herbal tea, and citrus herbal tea.

Here are some other tips with regard to tea:

- Cups should be preheated.

- The teapot should be heated before making the tea.

- A silver tea strainer is the classiest accessory for the table. In lieu of the external strainer, screened strainers that fit inside the pot are widely available.

- Ask the guest whether he or she prefers milk or lemon *while taking the order*, not after the tea has been delivered.

- Milk means milk, not half and half or cream.

- If the guest runs out of tea, offer an extra pot of hot water—there's usually some life left in the tea leaves.

- Attractive (and neat) honey service is rare, and very nice to have. A honey dipper or nondripping pourer can make a guest's life easier.

- Make sure the pits have been removed from the lemon, and don't put the lemon on a doily—doilies are meant for dry items.

Special attention paid to our coffee and tea lovers will pay off in the long run. Fine details get noticed and appreciated, and they are another sign of how far the restaurateur will go to please the guest.

THE BEVERAGE SIDE

THERE IS A LOT OF MONEY TO BE MADE WITH BEVERAGES; if you believe the numbers, most restaurants' beverage sales are from 25 to 30 percent of their gross sales. When you consider that the staff requirements to run a great beverage program are much lower than those required to produce the food that's served, and the fact that beverage cost is usually quite a bit lower than food cost, you can see that beverage service is a potential moneymaker if you run it right. Alcoholic beverage sales are also an area of great responsibility. In more ways than one, it pays to do it right.

CHAPTER 8:
STAFFING
CHALLENGES

People come to a restaurant to eat and drink, of course, but it's the ability of the staff to accommodate the guests' needs that can turn the dining experience into something truly special . . . or an experience the guest won't want to repeat. Labor is also the biggest expense in most restaurants, more than rent or food or beverage costs. So it's worth paying special attention to staffing issues.

Proper staffing of a restaurant, both back and front of the house, is a constant struggle. There have to be enough cooks for the kitchen to run efficiently, but not so many that they fall over each other. The wait staff needs to be big enough to handle busy shifts, but what happens when there is a slow night or even a slow season?

HIRING AND TRAINING

FINDING GOOD PEOPLE

Possibly the most important part of the staffing process is choosing the people who will work for you. The hiring process is a complex one and needs to be concentrated on two characteristics of the person being interviewed: skill and personality. These two aspects are important for both front- and back-of-the-house personnel, even though it might seem that skill is more important in a cook and personality is more important in a waiter.

The interview is an opportunity to discuss the person's skill level but is even more powerfully a chance to see what his or her personality is. Handshake, eye contact, and general demeanor are all to be judged objectively, but at some point you have to decide if this is a nice person sitting across the table from you.

I ASKED ANTHONY SCOTTO, of the New York restaurant Fresco by Scotto, "How long does it take before you know that you're going to hire someone in an interview?" He said, "Two minutes—but I'm still checking their last reference."

With personality determined, the candidate's skill level should be tested. Cooks should be given a chance to trail in the kitchen to show their abilities as well as their work ethic. Dining room staff should also have a chance to trail during service so they can show their skill level as well. If the applicant makes it through these tests, it's time to check references. While the person you're calling is only allowed legally to tell you whether the employee was punctual and worked assigned shifts, it's usually pretty easy to sense whether or not the applicant was a good employee, and then act on that information.

GETTING NEW EMPLOYEES UP TO SPEED

Once the right people have been hired, it is of critical importance that they receive proper training. In the old days, a waiter would get hired, come in and trail a veteran for a day or two, and then get thrown into the fray. It's obvious to most professionals today that this is not an effective method. The two main parts of any training program involve information and procedures.

INFORMATION

The most obvious information new employees need to have involves the menu and wine list, of course. Waiters must have a deep knowledge of the products being sold at the restaurant. Beyond that, the staff needs to know table numbers, seat positions, flatware settings for dishes—even the names of the owner and the background of the chef can prove useful. An easy-to-understand training manual should be written and maintained by the management. When each new hire comes in, the person should be required to read it, sign off on the fact that he or she read it, and then be tested on the information. In fact, it's smart to test the whole staff occasionally to keep them on their toes.

ON CHECKING REFERENCES

PAUL MCLAUGHLIN, general manager of Oceana in New York City, notes, "A number of years ago, I had an applicant who had been a captain at the Four Seasons. Nice fellow; he seemed like a fairly sophisticated guy. I called over there and I got the general manager on the phone. We chatted for a couple of minutes, then I said, 'Alex, I'm really calling to find out about this fellow who's applying for a job. Can you give me a little background on him?' There was a long pause, and then I said, 'Alex? I'm sorry, did you hear me?' He said, 'Oh, yes, Paul, I heard you.'"

PROCEDURES

The new waiter should be allowed to observe service with no tasks required at first. Specific veteran employees can be selected as trainers, and the new hire can learn from them. Yes, the trainees are learning specific ways of doing things, but they are also getting a sense of the house style from an old hand.

Most importantly, training should be planned, consistent, and documented for each new hire. A manager should be confident that if a waiter is working on the floor, he or she has sufficient knowledge of the operation. Knowing that everyone on the floor has the knowledge and training to do the job allows the manager to concentrate on the guests rather than worry about the staff.

Constant scrutiny of how well a particular staffing plan is working and subsequent adjustments are essential. Still, managers are dealing with multiple pressures, and the job of scheduling a large restaurant staff is not for the faint-hearted. The owner wants a seemingly impossible convergence of low labor cost with optimal staffing levels. The dining room employees want to work the best shifts, but they also want days off to go to the dentist or to an audition. The manager is the one who has to resolve all these tensions. I don't particularly enjoy scheduling, but to some people it can seem like a real-life chess game: "I'll give you next Thursday off if you work Sunday brunch." Of course, as soon as a schedule gets posted, negotiations between staffers and the manager are likely to start all over again.

WATCHING THE NUMBERS

THERE ARE TWO CATEGORIES OF NUMBERS to watch closely with regard to staffing—the volume of customers to be served and labor cost. The number of guests is important as a gauge of how much work there is to do, and it will also give you an estimated gross sales figure. Labor cost is determined, of course, by how many person-hours are being paid, and the number of managers on salary. Too many waiters and managers for the amount of business? Labor cost will be too high. Labor cost seems too low to be true? There's a good chance that there aren't enough people to get the job done, with food and service quality perhaps not what they should be and an overworked, stressed-out staff.

If the restaurant is brand new, there isn't any history to go on. So common sense comes into play, and you write a schedule that starts with a light staff on Monday, gradually building up to a full staff on Saturday. Then you get killed on the following Tuesday because no one knew that it was the town's annual Twilight Taco Festival and everybody came in for margaritas. An entry is made in the logbook with regard to this special evening so it doesn't happen again next year (see the section "Logbook" below).

Once patterns have developed, the manager can rely on at least ballpark figures when planning the schedule. In the absence of special events that can have a pronounced effect on the number of covers (Mother's Day increases volume, the Super Bowl lowers it), there are bound to be some days that are busier than others. New York's Wall Street financial district, for instance, is a ghost town on weekends, and during the week most activity ceases there after cocktail hour. In some suburban restaurants, the only times worth being open are Wednesday through Friday

PATTY, A FORMER WAITER at EJ's Luncheonette on the Upper West Side of Manhattan, says, "Ninety percent of the time, we waiters would rather be understaffed than overstaffed. Most of us didn't mind a hard day's work rather than having too many waiters for the business at hand."

ONE EXCEPTION TO THE RULE of not being open during slow times is when the ownership is trying to develop a niche clientele. The Blue Ribbon Restaurant in New York's Soho district is open (with a full menu) from 4 p.m. until 4 a.m. At first it was a little quiet in the wee hours. Eventually, though, workers at other restaurants in the area found out that there was a nice, cozy restaurant and bar that was open late enough for them to get a beer and a burger (or foie gras or matzoh ball soup) before heading home. I would arrive there at two in the morning after closing my restaurant, only to find the likes of Mario Batali and Bobby Flay there, having a late-night snack. To a certain degree, the place became a sort of after-hours clubhouse for restaurateurs. Other folks, of course, were discovering the place at the same time, and soon the restaurant was buzzing with activity until well past four in the morning. Obviously, it has paid off for the owners, the Bromberg brothers, and their extended restaurant family. They now have a bakery, two sushi restaurants, and another Blue Ribbon in Brooklyn. The late-night business might not be the only reason for their success, but their drive to stay open late, even when there wasn't much business, speaks volumes for their level of professional determination.

nights and weekends. Each restaurant will fall into a routine that can be relied upon (at least within sensible limits) to help predict business levels during a normal week. These patterns, of course, need to be monitored closely because they will change with time. A new parking garage in the area or a renovated theater across the street, for instance, can change everything. In order to make intelligent decisions with regard to predicted levels of business, you have to have good information. One invaluable source of that information is a well-maintained logbook, backed up with past reservation information.

LOGBOOK

TO STAFF THE RESTAURANT PROPERLY, you need to know how much business you'll be doing. For the first year or so, educated guesses are the best you can do, but if you have taken good notes during that year, you'll have a body of knowledge that can be relied upon (within reason) to help you to have the right number of waiters on the floor and cooks in the kitchen. Here are some of the categories to track, and the reasons to do so:

- **NUMBER OF COVERS.** An easily accessed record of the number of guests served is hugely important.

- **WEATHER.** You wrote a schedule for February based on last year's numbers ... but last year there was a three-day blizzard. Keep a record of temperature and precipitation (or lack thereof).

- **SPECIAL EVENTS AND HOLIDAYS.** Just as with the fictional Twilight Taco Festival example, special events can change the amount of business you'll get. Keep notes on local celebrations as well as national and religious holidays.

- **MANAGER ON DUTY.** Knowing which manager was at the restaurant on a certain day can help when you need the finer details of firsthand knowledge.

Of course, there are other categories that can be added to the logbook pages: accidents involving guests or employees, staffing levels, private room usage ... anything that can help you to make decisions in the future. The four bulleted items above should be the bare minimum, though. Remember, to make good decisions, a manager needs good information.

OUTDOOR CAFÉ STAFFING

MY FIRST MANAGEMENT JOB was at the Edward Moran Bar and Grill in downtown Manhattan. It was designed as a seventy-seat pub with outdoor seating for about the same. So on a beautiful summer day we could have 140 seats up and running. On a day that started out rainy, we couldn't use the outdoor seats, of course, so to save on labor cost I would send half of the wait staff home and concentrate on the indoor seating. Then the sun would come out ... as would everybody in downtown Manhattan who was hungry. Needless to say, we would all be out on the patio drying off the chairs and tables, and I would take a section or two—and not be able to do my job as manager.

The balancing act required by outdoor seating is a tricky one. It's important to have enough staff on hand to handle whatever level of business occurs, but you also have to keep the staff in mind with regard to both their income and the potential for boredom.

ATTILIO, MANAGER OF A FAMILY-STYLE ITALIAN RESTAURANT, comments, "The perfect balance on a schedule is when all the waiters have enough shifts so they can earn what they need, but with enough flexibility to get occasional needed days off. Of course, there are some work-horses who always want to handle a bigger load—just don't let them burn themselves out."

Here are some common difficulties with outdoor seating, and some solutions:

Problem: Waiters get tired of being sent home on a regular basis. After all, they have bills to pay, too.

Solution: Assign waiters to outside duty on a rotating basis.

Problem: In the spring and fall, the weather can be unpredictable at best. Veteran waiters aren't going to want to be sent away on a regular basis, even if the rotation is a fair one.

Solution: New waiters can be given more outdoor shifts than the waiters with seniority. As they accumulate more time on the job, they will get more of the most dependable shifts.

Problem: It looks like the skies are about to open and flood your entire patio. Waiters start jostling for position to take the rest of the day off. Who goes home?

Solution: Check an Internet weather site to see what the forecast is. Even better, find a Web site that has radar images to see what's coming your way. If a monsoon is about to hit, batten down the hatches and send most of the staff home. If it looks like it's going to be just a brief shower, tell the staff to relax for a few minutes until it blows over.

Problem: Indian summer arrives on an October weekday, and all the guests want to sit outside for the last time this year . . . but you staffed the restaurant for a normal fall afternoon.

Solution: Get the outdoor tables cleaned and set up *quickly,* then fill one section at a time, sending one waiter at a time outside to cover them.

Problem: It is pouring outside, and some of the waiters are going to be sent home. Who stays, who goes?

Solution: Well, it might have to come down to seniority, but why not just ask them first? Some waiters may want to go home anyway because they know that tips will be low or they have some personal matters they can attend to.

KITCHEN SCHEDULING

THE GOOD THING ABOUT SCHEDULING the cooks and other kitchen staff is that kitchen workers tend to have a steady schedule from week to week. They also tend to have the highest hourly wages in the place—cooks often make two or three times as much as tipped employees—and the slightest overstaffing can cost the house big bucks. While most kitchen staffs are scheduled by the chef or sous chef, the increased use of kitchen managers in the quick-service restaurant (QSR) sector means that more general managers are in charge of *all* scheduling than ever before.

If your accountant tells you that the kitchen labor cost is too high, you should resist the impulse to slash payroll by cutting the number of cooks' shifts drastically. To go from too many cooks to too few is not healthy for the restaurant. It is best to be analytical about staffing in the kitchen (and everywhere else, too) rather than reacting in a knee-jerk fashion to an accountant's report. Remember, the accountant might know numbers, but *you* know the restaurant biz. Small, thoughtful adjustments to the kitchen schedule are more easily monitored and evaluated than huge, sweeping changes. If you constantly overreact—cutting too much in response to balance-sheet issues, then scheduling too many shifts back in because food is coming out too slowly and guests are unhappy—it's hard to pinpoint what to correct. With smaller, incremental adjustments, the financial aspects can be analyzed on a week-by-week basis (by using weekly sales and payroll reports), and the operational side can be evaluated more thoroughly by watching how the staff works in different configurations from day to day. You won't know if something will work if you don't try it. If your first attempt doesn't work, change things back; if it does, you win.

NO-SHOWS AND SICK DAYS

WHEN AN EMPLOYEE DOESN'T SHOW UP FOR WORK, everybody suffers. Guests, co-workers, and managers all bear the brunt of no-shows—it's not likely going to be a very smooth service that day, and you may well have to begin a new employee search. Take no-shows seriously.

I often use somebody's no-show to let the staff members see what happens when someone doesn't turn up and doesn't call. The staffer who didn't show up is often remorseful and may either call to apologize or just show up for the next shift. The phrase that I like to use in this case is, "Well, when you didn't call or come in to work, I figured that you had resigned . . . technically, it's called 'willful abandonment of the workplace.'" There is occasionally a good enough reason for the failure to show up that you should take the employee back, but usually it's more prudent to let the person go and find someone new. The more often staff members can get away with no-shows, the less seriously the rest of the staff will take you as a manager.

I realize this may seem harsh and that it may feel much easier to let the employee come back to work, with the promise to yourself that he or she will be replaced when a new employee starts. There are a number of problems with this. First, a no-show means that there is an employee on your staff who probably shouldn't be there. If this person doesn't have enough respect for the workplace to call in, he or she probably shouldn't be working there. The lack of professionalism in this regard does not bode well for this person's professionalism during the shift, and professional behavior is what quality service is all about. The other major problem is the one mentioned above: when other staffers see that nothing really happens to workers who just don't show up, it either encourages others to do the same or discourages the good workers, who see that professionalism isn't rewarded, or at least that unprofessional behavior goes unpunished.

Besides, when a manager says he or she will replace someone "when it's more convenient," it's more likely that nothing will change. Sure, it seems like a good idea to let the person stay on for a while—who wants to write a whole new schedule and put half the staff on doubles? But the next week comes along, and you forgot that one of the captains is getting married and the maître d' is his best man. You can't fire the employee now, either—you need someone to fill those shifts. Eventually, the worker who willfully abandoned the workplace has slipped back into the staff. It may be better all around just to bite the bullet and let the person go.

Sick days are another story entirely. When someone is sick, he or she should stay home—both to get better and to avoid getting other workers (and guests) sick. If a staffer becomes conspicuous for calling in sick a lot, then it turns into a situation like that of the no-show—even if the sick days are valid, the worker is proving unreliable and might need to be replaced.

One way to deal with the problem of staffers not showing up is to create an on-call shift on the schedule. You can put one or two waiters on call each shift. Rotate through the staff to be fair, and have them call in to the restaurant by a certain time each day to see if they're needed.

TERMINATION AND SUSPENSION

WHEN THERE IS SOMEONE WORKING FOR YOU who shouldn't be, for one reason or another, it is usually best to deal with the consequences of letting that person go, whether that includes putting other staff on doubles or even picking up shifts yourself (which should be a last resort, because it means that you won't be able to properly supervise the multitude of things that need to get done).

Reasons for termination, especially immediate termination, must be printed in the employee manual; there's a reason that human-resources people want to get a signature from new employees signifying that they have read and understand the restaurant's policies. The policies that you come up with must, of course, be legal, and should be in full accordance with antidiscrimination laws. Here are some situations that often result in immediate termination:

- Use of drugs or alcohol during work hours, or the sale or trafficking in illegal substances in the workplace

- Physical violence directed at *anyone* on the restaurant's premises—guests, co-workers, vendors

- Illegal actions, such as theft, embezzlement, or credit card fraud

- Consistent incompetence—a series of well-documented deficiencies in work performance (here documentation is essential)

- Repeated unexcused tardiness or absence

- Failure to follow company policies regarding matters such as confidentiality and harassment

While the behaviors listed above should, obviously, result in termination, lesser acts of unprofessional behavior could be appropriately handled with either suspension or written reprimands. These forms of discipline should be reserved for employees who are worth saving, as either would only serve to draw out the process of letting someone go.

THE THREE-STRIKES POLICY

The three-strikes-and-you're-out policy has been used in several places where I have worked, and it is quite easy to administer. Each strike is an incident of unacceptable behavior.

1. The first strike results in a verbal warning.

2. The second strike results in a written warning, with a copy maintained in the employee's personnel file.

3. The third strike results in suspension or termination.

The beauty of this approach is that the employees have a chance to straighten things out, but if they don't, there is documentation of the behavior that might lead to termination. The key, of course, is consistency—not only in the way the infractions are documented, but also in that you can't just pick the employees that you want to get rid of and discipline them for behaviors that in other employees would be allowed to pass without any action. If your best bartender does something stupid, he or she must be disciplined just like the boneheaded waiter who was hired by the previous manager. Fairness like this is not only correct on moral grounds but also important so that the rest of the staff knows what the rules are and how the process works. In addition, it's vital for your defense in the case of a labor-related lawsuit.

HOSPITALITY FROM WITHIN

IT MIGHT SEEM disingenuous to talk about being nice to each other after this information on how to fire people, but in fact the best way to make sure that your restaurant runs as smoothly as possible is to make sure that everyone on the staff is happy. Treating the staff well creates an atmosphere in which they're willing to give their best on the job. And guests really do perceive (at least subconsciously) the positive atmosphere that results from a staff who feels they are treated fairly. It makes the restaurant feel like a place guests want to return to.

Creating a positive atmosphere isn't all mysterious alchemy. Here are some concrete suggestions:

- Your staff members don't have to be best friends, but it's nice when all of the personalities combine in a good way. Keep this idea in mind when hiring people, and if possible choose those who seem as though they have the right personality to fit in well.

- Having the right number of waiters on the floor means that everybody will be busy enough to make good money but won't be constantly in the weeds.

- Stability is important. We have enough excitement built into our business because of the public contact. Therefore, employees usually welcome predictability in the workplace. This predictability can take the form of consistent work schedules, low employee turnover (so you build relationships), and consistent, fair management.

- Benefits are key these days if you want to build a veteran staff. Health insurance, retirement plans, and professional development can often keep employees with you even if a rival restaurant offers a higher tip average.

- Throw a party for your staff. A holiday party in the winter and/or a picnic in the summer can work wonders for staff morale. Hold it on a day when the restaurant is usually closed, and have the management cook for and serve the staff. The boss in an apron usually gets a laugh or two, and the staff will not forget the gesture.

- Make the most of the restaurant's family meal. Feed your employees well, and they'll work hard for you. The quality of the food that we feed our own work family speaks volumes about how we value them.

Think about it this way—we send our staff out every night to face a whole bunch of complete strangers. It's their job to make these people happy, at almost any cost. But they won't be able to do that effectively if they're miserable themselves.

It's obvious to anyone in the restaurant business as well as to guests that some establishments exude the feeling that people aren't happy there. However, there are also restaurants that seem to shimmer with emotional warmth, and there's a good chance that this warmth has its source in the hearts of the staff. Our business is more than hard enough—shouldn't we be nice to each other? The kicker here is that being nice to each other has a financial benefit. Guests can feel the warmth and will be drawn to it, and you will soon have repeat business.

CHAPTER 9:
TAKING CARE OF
BUSINESS

The focus of this book is service and hospitality, and at first glance the business end of the restaurant world might not seem to have too much relevance to that larger theme. But it's important not to forget that hospitality is a business, and if it isn't run properly, with sufficient attention to the bottom line, none of us will have jobs.

I believe, based on twenty years in the restaurant world, that everyone who works in a restaurant should have some involvement with the financial side of the business. Service staff members do a better job when they understand at least a little about the business end of the dining room. It helps them understand why managers ask them to perform tasks in certain ways rather than others, and it helps them to see how each of their actions can contribute to the restaurant's bottom line, thereby making their jobs more secure.

Some people are drawn to accounting and enjoy working with numbers, while others would probably rather polish every single piece of flatware in the place rather than generate a profit-and-loss (P&L) statement. A good manager will find a way to get the second group interested in the numbers generated by the first.

There are several ways for a manager to help the staff to become financially savvy.

- Share financial information with middle management—either a full P&L, or just the numbers for the department in question.

WHILE IT ISN'T AS ESSENTIAL to the financial health of the restaurant, it is good to get the accountants or business managers involved in the operations of the restaurant. It's great for them to gain firsthand knowledge of the products and jobs that they usually see only on a piece of paper or computer screen. This knowledge helps by giving them the whole picture to work with rather than just one aspect. Remember the story about a group of blind men describing an elephant? To involve the financial staff in operations, you could put them through the waiter training program. If there isn't enough time to do that, have the money people spend some evenings at the front desk with the maître d' or host so that they can see dining room operations from the catbird's seat. Failing that, at least have your accountant sit down for a meal in the restaurant from time to time.

THE STRUCTURE OF A MANAGEMENT TEAM depends largely on the size and complexity of the restaurant. In some small restaurants, the owner is the only manager, but in larger operations there is often a general manager, dining room or service manager, beverage manager, and assistant managers, who should all have a stake in financial success of the restaurant. In the kitchen, there is a similar structure, with the executive chef in charge of the whole food operation, the chef de cuisine to run the kitchen, and then various sous chefs to manage smaller aspects of the kitchen.

- Build bonus structures to reward employees who keep costs in line. This could range from rewarding a waiter who figures out how to save money on iced tea to giving a bonus to the manager who lowers your liquor cost.

- During the managers' annual reviews, set specific and achievable financial goals—for example, to keep overtime under a set dollar amount.

- Ask all employees and managers for cost-cutting suggestions. If two heads are better than one, how about a whole bunch of heads? General managers often forget how smart their staff is and that the employees also care about the financial health of the workplace.

- If the restaurant is on shaky ground financially, don't try to keep it a secret from the managers involved—rumors can be much worse than the truth.

Now, from this somewhat general advice on how to get the staff involved, let's move on to somewhat more specific areas.

PRODUCT COSTS

THE FRONT-OF-THE-HOUSE MANAGER usually has little if anything to do with managing the food products that go into the kitchen, but beverages and other items used in the front of the house, such as linen, are almost always that manager's direct responsibility.

BEVERAGES

With beverage sales accounting for 20–30 percent of restaurant sales nationwide, the proper management of a beverage program can have a huge impact, either positive or negative, on the financial health of a restaurant.

CONTROLLING THE PRODUCT

On my first day on a new job as beverage manager, the owner said to me, "I don't understand how we can be losing money. Wine and bar sales are great, and we're getting great volume discounts on wine and liquor, but we just aren't making money!" I asked to see a copy of the sales report, the purchase log, and the inventory. He gave me the first two, then said, "Here's the inventory from when we opened. We haven't done anything since then—it's such a pain." At that point I knew what the problem was.

Wine and liquor presumably leave your restaurant inside of your paying customers. Almost any other way is the wrong way. It is the job of a beverage manager to be fully aware of the comings and goings of liquor, wine, and beer bottles.

It's an unfortunate reality of the restaurant business that there are dishonest employees and managers out there. The most important control is to watch the numbers closely, with the key tools being sales reports, invoices, and the inventory sheets. Additionally, it's easier than ever to install security cameras in places of business, and I highly recommend their use. Make sure that there is always a recording device attached to it, and that the videos get watched. While the visibility of the cameras will slow down theft to a certain degree, the true power of surveillance will be unrealized unless someone watches the tapes.

While employee theft is something to be watched out for, it is far more important to concentrate on the daily operations of the restaurant. The occasional loss of product or money to a dishonest worker can be far overshadowed by the steady leakage of a poorly run beverage program.

PURCHASING AND RECEIVING

Smart buying procedures along with systems that ensure proper handling of received product are the beginning of a solid beverage program.

The beverage manager should do his or her best to purchase wisely. Once the order has been placed, it is important for the restaurant to be prepared for its arrival, which often will be the next day.

Make sure there is somebody available to receive the delivery. Just as someone must check food deliveries to make sure the ordered amount is present, the prices are as agreed upon, and the food is of good quality, these same tasks must be carried out with beverage deliveries as well. If you ordered five cases of the house Champagne for delivery on Friday but only one shows up, there might be some problems during the weekend. Making sure that what is delivered matches the invoice is also of vital importance, as once the delivery has been accepted by the restaurant, fixing the problem becomes much more difficult.

Here are some categories of information that should be part of any document that is used for receiving beverage deliveries:

- Description of the item, including the name of the producer, name of the wine, the vintage year, color of the wine, vineyard designation (if necessary), and size of bottle (375 ml, 750 ml, or 1.5 L, for example)

- Number of cases

- Number of bottles per case (most wines come packed twelve bottles to a case, but some come in so-called six-packs)

- Expected temperature upon arrival (overheated wine has probably been damaged beyond repair)

- Expected time of arrival (deliveries should not be planned or accepted during lunch or dinner service)

- Wholesale prices, including any discounts

- Name of distributor

All of this information should be grouped by delivery, and cross-referenced at the bottom, so that the receiver has an idea of how many cases will be coming in that morning—it's good to know beforehand that twenty cases of wine are coming in.

Incidentally, the person doing the receiving should be someone other than the person placing the order. If they are one and the same, there is potential for problems; for example, the person could order extra and then claim that it didn't come in. The truth emerges eventually, but in the meantime someone is stealing. In most smaller restaurants, there isn't enough staff to split up responsibilities; in such cases there really isn't much you can do other than develop trust within the management.

Once the invoice has been signed, the product must be stored securely within the premises. Cases of liquor and wine cannot sit out on the sidewalk unattended. This product now belongs to the house and is part of your inventory.

INVENTORY

One of the most common problems with beverage programs involves the inventory. Workers especially, but also sometimes managers and owners, tend to forget that all of the wine, liquor, beer, and nonalcoholic beverages in the restaurant are money. Everything in the house either has been or will be paid for by the owner or management. Every bottle of beer, can of pineapple juice, and maraschino cherry represents someone's cash. Just as we count the money in the safe every day, the property of the restaurant needs to be counted on a regular basis. This is especially true of food and beverage because they turn over so rapidly.

The conceptual areas that are the most important to the validity of an inventory document are frequency, timing, and accuracy. Frequency, or how often the inventory is taken, is flexible. However, it should be taken at least on a monthly basis. Monthly inventories should coincide with monthly sales reports so that the documents can reinforce each other if needed for analysis. Of course, inventory can be taken more frequently, depending on the circumstances. In some restaurants weekly inventories work best, and in the most problematic cases you may need to do it daily until the actual and predicted inventory numbers are close enough every time. Then you can back off to weekly and eventually monthly inventories once the situation is under control.

Why can actual inventory vary so much from what the invoices and sales records would suggest it should be? It can be one of a large number of variables, but the overarching problem is sloppiness. Taking inventory regularly is important. Also, having employees know about the process and why it's being done helps workers to understand that they need to be as accurate as possible.

Accuracy goes hand in hand with frequency. The smallest slip—a case of wine missed, a bin counted twice—can throw the numbers off enough to cause concern in the main office. Bartenders count their cash drawer at least twice—why not the bottles in the liquor room as well? A case of vodka can be worth $200—the full amount of some cash drawers.

Taking inventory requires sufficient time and concentration. An employee who tries to do the inventory with a friend there or while listening to Led Zeppelin's "Kashmir" on an MP3 player will not be attending fully to the task at hand. Similarly, the bar manager who zips through the bar stock in record time because she wants to make it home to watch the seventh game of the World Series is likely to make mistakes. Whoever does the counting needs to concentrate on the task at hand and take the time to do it right.

One familiar model to use when counting bottles is for one person to "read," or count, the product while the other writes the numbers down. This can break the mind-numbing monotony of doing inventory locked up in the basement by yourself. Also, it takes less time and can increase reliability.

Timing can make a difference in how easy it is to reconcile all your inputs. The best time to count product is after the end of business on the last night of the month, before business starts on the first day of the new month. That way, the sales reports that are spewed out by the point-of-sale computer can be reconciled directly with the inventory for that month. This makes it easier to track down inconsistencies and figure out why they're occurring. Doing this monthly also gives you a coherent set of numbers that you can use to track trends over time more easily, within the parameters set by the owner or business manager.

CONTROLLING CONSUMABLES

THERE ARE MANY items used in service that have to be ordered on a regular basis because they get used, or used up, during the process of taking care of guests. The two main categories are items intended for single use and those that are used repeatedly but eventually wear out or break. In both cases, it is important to conserve the resources rather than squander them.

SINGLE-USE ITEMS

LINEN

Of all single-use items, one of the most costly for fine dining establishments is table linens. Most restaurants rent linens from a linen company, and it's not inexpensive, as I noted in Chapter 4. It's relatively simple to control linen costs if the whole staff helps. If you don't point out what it costs, kitchen staff will think nothing of using napkins as side towels, and the dining room staff may toss a freshly cleaned but stained tablecloth right into the dirty-linen bag instead of returning it to the linen service for credit. It takes both training and vigilance on the part of the manager to avoid such occurrences. Here are some other tips to help control your linen costs:

- Put a bin for unacceptable linens to be returned to the linen company in a place that is easily accessible to the floor staff. The less they have to walk, the more they'll do it.

- Don't let waiters and bussers use clean or dirty table linens to clean up spills—if the linen company considers linens beyond reuse, you will get charged for them.

- For the same reason, don't let cooks use napkins as side towels. Even though they are less expensive than side towels, napkins are intended for less aggressive purposes than towels and under punishing conditions will have a shorter life span. Damaged napkins will end up costing more than properly used side towels.

- Store linen in a clean, dry place. Keep it organized and folded properly so it doesn't become wrinkled and thus unusable.

- Have a staff person receive linens, just as you would perishables and beverages. There's a lot of money on the line.

- Keep a close eye on the quality of the linen as it comes in. Linen companies need to be kept honest, just as a food purveyor does. If they know that you are on top of the situation, they are less likely to try to slip something by you.

- Polyester and blends cost less to rent than 100 percent cotton, but my personal opinion is that they feel cheap and aren't worth the cost savings. Charge another quarter for each menu item and use cotton. You can, however, save money by using polyester tablecloths as underliners beneath the topcloth. If you line trays or shelves with linen, this is also a good place for man-made fabrics.

- A very small number of restaurants buy their linens and do the laundry themselves. The labor cost of doing this is quite high, but the degree of control that you have over the final product is the benefit.

Whatever methods you choose to control linen costs, the key word is control. A linen program left to its own devices will seek its own, very expensive level.

BREAD AND BUTTER

Although bread and its various possible accompaniments are foodstuffs, usually they're the responsibility of the front of the house. While some restaurateurs consider bread a necessary commodity and not much more, others recognize how influential the quality of the bread and butter (or olive oil, or Tuscan white bean spread) is in the guests' perception of the restaurant. These items can show how much a restaurant cares about its guests.

Unfortunately, good bread isn't cheap. Neither is good butter or olive oil. The key to saving money in this area is, of course, careful management. In this case, the idea is (as with linen) to monitor the staff's use of these items and to keep the products from being wasted. For example, many waiters and bussers will try to save time by slicing all of the bread before service begins. Of course, guests in later seatings will, by definition, receive stale sliced bread, but the other wasteful aspect is that once the bread has been sliced, it can no longer be saved for later use, either fresh or frozen. All of that presliced bread goes into the trash at the end of the night. Other things to watch out for:

- The amount of bread in the basket should be relative to the number of guests at the table. Too much, and bread gets thrown away.

- Waiters should not overload the basket in order to avoid extra trips. If a guest gets the proper amount and wants more, the waiter gets more (and probably less than what usually counts as a full bread basket).

- Butter should also be delivered to the table in measured quantities.

- Either olive oil can be poured by the waiter or a bottle of it can be left on the table for the guests' use. If the waiter pours for everyone, portion size can be controlled, but some guests may not want it, and so the oil that's already poured goes to waste. The solution is to have the waiter ask each guest if he or she would like oil. You can also leave the bottle on the table, but some guests will go overboard and use gallons. If you do this, figure the increased cost into the restaurant's food cost.

- Those in the know are aware that top-quality bread should be served at room temperature, but some guests want hot bread. However, reheated bread goes stale faster, and if it's unused, it usually has to be thrown out at the end of the night. The answer is to serve at bread room temperature and warm it up for those who request it.

- If you put the bread basket on the table as soon as the guests sit down, they may fill up on your wonderful bread and not order as much from the menu. So you might want to change your sequence of service and serve bread after the order has been taken. In more luxurious restaurants, though, you aren't as worried about people ordering enough food, so you can still serve the bread before the order has been taken.

- Do not be tempted to reuse bread or butter that comes back from a table. It's illegal, it's disgusting, and it can make people very sick. If the bread is managed properly, the amount returned from the tables will be minimal.

Any arguments from staff people that the methods above make their jobs harder should be answered with an explanation of both the quality and fiscal issues that are being attended to with your suggested approach.

MULTIPLE-USE ITEMS

GLASSWARE

Glasses break—some more easily than others. Generally, stemware is the most fragile. Other aspects that make breakage more likely are the thinness of the glass, whether it is crystal or not, and how thin the rim of the glass is. These variables are important to keep in mind, but a healthy amount of fatalism comes in handy as well; there is going to be breakage, and the costs of it have to be planned for. The cost of doing business is rarely more apparent than when a full rack of Riedel or Spiegelau glasses takes a dive and you hear a $300 crash.

There are some ways to cut down on unnecessary breakage. One of the most overlooked details is having proper glass racks for the dishwashing machine. If the compartments in the rack are too narrow, the glasses have to be forced in, and can break. If the compartments are too wide, the glasses can rattle around inside them while in the machine, allowing them to get marked up or perhaps broken. If the rack is too shallow and the bases of the glasses stick out above the top of the rack, anyone who places another rack on top can break off the base of every single glass in the bottom rack.

Once the correct racks are being used, the stacks of dirty glasses in racks should not be so high that they are top-heavy. Similarly, waiters who are polishing or moving clean glasses around should not be allowed to stack the racks high enough that they become unstable. In this case, it's not just the cost of the glasses at stake, it's also the safety of your staff.

Every staff member who works with glassware should be made aware of the costs involved. It isn't right, in my opinion, to make staff pay for breakage that took place at their hands, but the employee should know exactly how much it is costing the restaurant so that it's less likely to happen again.

Increased care taken by the staff, using the proper equipment in the handling of glassware, and an acceptance of the inevitability of accidents are all important aspects to maintain this area of your equipment inventory properly.

CHINA AND FLATWARE

China and flatware are not as easily broken as glass, but of course dishes can get broken from time to time, and pieces of flatware sometimes get thrown into the garbage. Here's how to help prevent those problems.

Usually plate breakage occurs because of mishandling. A cook or waiter will try to carry too many at once, the stack will be wet and slippery, or a stack of them will be either badly positioned on a shelf or stacked too high. The issue of safety is again intermingled with that of fiscal responsibility, so it is important to monitor the work habits of the staff with regard to the handling of this category of restaurant equipment. As with glassware, it is important for the workers to know the value of the equipment they work with.

Flatware sometimes winds up in the garbage because it's concealed under the contents of the plate, or because the waiter or busser sees it go in during scraping but doesn't want to reach it and pick it out. There are contraptions designed to stop or slow the loss of flatware, such as big magnets that sit atop the waste bin, poised to catch the metal pieces on their way past. Unfortunately, they also catch unwanted metal pieces (such as bottle caps) and get gummed up with food refuse very quickly. I consider them a waste of time and money, but go ahead and try one if you want.

I think it's better to get the staff to improve their habits. Their desire to do the right thing should be enough to help that happen. It helps, too, if they know how expensive quality flatware can be. If this doesn't work and losses are excessive, it may be necessary to delegate staffers to go through the garbage with rubber gloves on a rotating basis—but it won't be necessary for long, as employees will see how preferable it is to prevent the problem before it occurs.

LABOR COSTS

AS WE'VE NOTED, the greatest expense in the restaurant business is not exotic ingredients or specialized equipment, but payroll. It's true that many dining room employees receive a fairly low hourly wage and make the bulk of their money from tips, but those hourly wages do add up. Plus you must consider the wages of the nontipped employees, such as kitchen staff, and the costs of benefits for both groups. Then there are other expenses, such as the cost of family meals. There are a few tricks you can use to help cut these costs down to size, however.

OVERTIME

Two of your waiters are standing in front of you. One of them should not be there—the one who has worked more than forty hours that week. Both waiters are doing the same job, but your overtime worker is costing you 50 percent more than the other one. It isn't worth it, and overtime can usually be avoided with proper hiring, training, and scheduling. When it is impossible to avoid, such as because of a worker calling in sick or an especially busy time of year, send the overtime worker home as soon as possible to cut down on excessive payroll costs. Whatever you do, don't agree to let staffers work off the clock (and certainly don't force them to). It's against the law, and you will eventually get caught.

The above information goes double for your wage-only earners. A host making $15 an hour normally costs you $120 for an eight-hour shift, but every time that person works a sixth day, the daily cost rises to $180. Simply put, overtime is just wasteful—it's bad business.

Here are some tips that will help you to maximize the productivity of your staff. First of all, try to get tipped employees to do some of the work that nontipped employees usually take care of. For example, if you put some housekeeping work into waiters' setup and running cleanups (such as cleaning the glass in the front doors during service), there is less cleaning for the porter to do. Don't overload the waiters, but if they can do some of this during the times when they are least busy and would otherwise be standing around, you can save some money.

The flip side of that strategy is to have salaried employees do some of the work that is normally the province of hourly or tipped employees. Now, you can't exactly have managers taking tables during service, because that precludes them from actually managing the restaurant. But those same managers and other salaried staff (such as office managers and kitchen management) can do inventory and other chores that would cost you a bundle if the head bartender or host did them. Again, you don't want to insist that they add additional responsibilities if they're already working at full capacity, and especially not if they're overburdened—that's a sure way to generate resentment. But if it's possible, it's a good idea.

Managing people well and profitably is not easy. It requires both a firm hand and compassion—two qualities that aren't always found in the same person. Consider a situation in which business is slow and some of the waiters have to go home for the night with no money. A good manager will ask first if anyone wants to go home. If nobody wants to leave, that same manager can have the staff draw straws, or possibly send home the workers with the least seniority. Additionally, the manager should explain to the staff the reasons for sending people home—too many waiters standing around doing nothing, none of the waiters will make much money if everyone stays, and so on. Make decisions fairly, explain them to the staff, and be consistent and firm—it works.

PROACTIVE BUSINESS MANAGEMENT

THERE ARE MANAGERS THE WORLD OVER who are just as happy when business is slow in the restaurant as when it's humming. They can usually go home earlier, it doesn't take as much time to place orders, and the workday is generally less stressful, with fewer guests to take care of. This is all well and good until the bills can't get paid, the restaurant goes out of business, and the manager is looking for another job.

A good manager (or owner) will take slow business periods and make something happen to bring in more money.

TRADITIONALLY SLOW PERIODS

Summer at a ski resort, winter in a seaside town—these aren't exactly boom times for restaurants in those locales, but with some creative thought, there is money to be made. The ski resort, for instance, could host a weeklong mountain bike racing event that could bring people from miles around. A seaside town could host a food-centered festival that takes place in several indoor locales.

Speaking of winter, it's the perfect time in most temperate regions to have wine-oriented dinners, partly because things are pretty slow at most wineries and the winemaker is often available for personal visits, which can entice guests to sign up for the event. Another way to entice guests to come to the restaurant during a traditionally slow period is to lower prices—a bargain prix-fixe dinner with wines by the glass paired with each course can fill a restaurant on Monday nights.

Whatever method you choose, there must be a perceived value to draw in the guests—lower prices, lecture programs, free wine, cooking lessons. Some owners recoil at the thought of giving the house away, but would they rather have four people paying full price or a restaurant full of guests who are paying somewhat less per head? It's the latter that will pay more bills.

CHECK AVERAGES

The previous section suggests lower prices as one way to bring customers into the house. However, during normal business periods, a higher check average is good business. There are certain fixed costs incurred for each guest served, so increasing sales per guest will lower the cost of doing business. There are ways to increase sales without being pushy, and most of them require some effort on the staff's part as well as yours. A few suggestions:

- Offer wine training for the staff. The more comfortable the staff is with the wine list, the more wine they will sell, mostly because it will be easier for them to figure out what the guest wants.

- Make it easy to order wine. As discussed in Chapter 7, the simpler you make it for the guests to buy wine, the more wine you will sell. Streamline the list and make it easy to read, or if a hallmark of your restaurant is its extensive wine list, hire a sommelier.

- Keep savory food portion sizes under control. Dessert sales will be higher as a result.

- Promote the sales of low-alcohol aperitifs. At the end of the meal, the guest will have consumed less alcohol, and you can sell them a digestif or dessert wine without overserving them.

- Sell restaurant-themed retail items. Clothing with the logo of the restaurant, pepper mills, and wineglasses are some of the items that you can have available for sale. (I even sold one of our chairs to a customer once—I got a good price for it, too.)

- Create a before-dinner menu of food to be eaten with cocktails. Olives and roasted almonds are good choices. At Fresco by Scotto in Manhattan, they sell potato and zucchini chips with melted Gorgonzola that are completely addictive—and you'll see them on almost every table.

Whatever is done to increase the per-guest sales, make sure that the staff isn't pushy about it—guests can detect a hard sell from miles away, which will keep them miles away from your restaurant.

INTELLIGENT DILIGENCE

THIS CHAPTER BOILS DOWN to a fairly simple premise: the flow of money into and out of your restaurant must be watched closely. Sales come through the in door; purchases, payroll, insurance, rent, and all other expenses head through the out door. It is imperative that every dollar leaving your place is well spent. It doesn't mean that you have to be a miser—just be smart with your money. Having the restaurant on a sound financial footing makes for a more relaxed atmosphere overall. The staff feels the difference, and so will the customers—they'll want to come back.

CHAPTER 10:
IT'S GOING TO HAPPEN: HANDLING EMERGENCIES

It really is just a matter of time—there will be an emergency in your restaurant. Our business is a patchwork of open flames, boiling water, sharp knives, and slippery floors. Looking at it that way, I'm surprised that there aren't more emergency situations in restaurants. While nearly anything can happen, there are three main categories that emergencies can be sorted into: bad things that happen to guests, bad things that happen to employees, and bad things that happen to the facility. There is, of course, some crossover between categories, but I think that it makes sense to delineate them this way, because each of these types of problems should be handled somewhat differently.

GUEST EMERGENCIES

GUESTS ARE USUALLY STRANGERS TO US. We don't know whether they have any preexisting health conditions, and in today's litigious society it can even be risky to help someone, which I think is a darn shame. Nonetheless, most restaurant personnel unhesitatingly jump in to assist when a patron has an emergency. I have found that instinct usually takes over when adversity arrives, but it helps to have a plan.

While physical injury and illness account for most of the bad things that happen to guests, they arrive in different forms, which require different handling.

SLIPS AND FALLS

The floors are clean. There is slip-prevention tape on every step of every staircase in the place, and the bar has brand-new carpeting. Still, a guest will, at some point, take a fall in the restaurant. More than once I have seen customers slip and fall on a perfectly dry, clean, unvarnished wood floor. It might not make sense, but it's going to happen.

When someone has fallen, don't move him or her. The first thing to do is to ask the guest if he or she is okay, without letting the person stand up. As the guest slowly gets up, follow first-aid precautions and give the person a chance to check his or her extremities for injury. In a busy restaurant, this might even mean directing traffic around the downed guest.

Usually the guest's pride has taken the worst hit, in that it's not much fun to be the center of attention while lying on the floor of a busy restaurant. If there is any suspicion of physical injury, though, paramedics should be called immediately. It's not worth taking the risk of either letting the guest go home, only to find that he or she is really hurt, or trying to treat the injury yourself. This is not solely to avoid liability—it's to have the job handled by health care professionals, who can be more effective.

If the guest professes to be uninjured, you should still get the person's name, phone number, and mailing address, and log the accident in the logbook. There should also be incident forms available at the front desk of the restaurant so that the manager has ready access to them. The more (and better) records you keep of the incident, the better prepared you'll be if the guest decides to sue you.

ILLNESS

If a guest gets sick because of something you gave him or her, it's probably due either to toxicity (food poisoning) or to allergy. Either way, the paramedics should be called immediately. One bright spot is that people with food allergies are usually very careful when ordering food because of the potential for severe illness if they eat something they shouldn't. Also, they will often carry an EpiPen or other medical device to avoid anaphylactic shock from a food allergy; while not a cure, it gives a self-deliverable dose of epinephrine that can give health professionals some more time to treat the patient. Common food allergies include peanuts, tree nuts (walnuts, pecans, etc.), shellfish, fish, milk, soy, wheat, and eggs. Because some food allergies can potentially lead to fatality, the staff must take the subject seriously. Waiters need to know the ingredients in various dishes not only to be able to describe them to guests but, in this case, to avoid doing harm to them as well. The above list has the most important items to be aware of, but there are more. Any time a guest asks about certain ingredients, the waiter must assume that there could be an allergy

THERE IS A DIFFERENCE between food poisoning and food illness. Food poisoning (toxicity) occurs when there is a toxin (such as botulinum toxin) present in the food. This will cause the guest to feel ill immediately. Foodborne illness, however, occurs when a bacteria (such as salmonella) or virus in the food gets into the guest's system and reproduces to the point where it makes the guest sick. This can take time to develop, and so is rarely the reason for a guest to feel ill at the restaurant.

situation and know the answer. If he or she isn't sure, the waiter *must* check with someone in the kitchen regarding the ingredient. Lastly, if no one in the kitchen has a solid answer, advise the guest not to order the dish in question.

Toxicity issues are trickier to discern, but in case of any apparent guest illness, professional health care providers should be called immediately.

INJURY FROM FOREIGN OBJECTS IN FOOD

Unfortunately, foreign objects will sometimes make it into food and onto the guest's plate. Some of the surprise ingredients that guests have made me aware of include bugs, broken glass, twist ties, big metal staples from produce boxes, pieces of pot-scrubbing pads, Band-Aids, hair, rocks, nut shells, and plastic wrap. Some of these items could lead to choking, and others could obviously injure the guest—I have seen broken teeth, cut lips, and cut tongues.

Every one of these cases was a delicate situation because, while accidental, the injury was still inflicted by the restaurant. It is important, as with other emergencies, to give first aid if appropriate, call professional health care, and document the incident. One cannot help feeling bad when guests get hurt by something we gave them. The inherent trust that they have in us has been violated. It is up to us to gain that trust back by getting them the medical help they need and handling the business end properly. Depending on the severity of the situation, the monetary solution can range from taking the befouled menu item off the check to buying their entire meal. On the medical side, professionals should handle anything beyond a minor injury. As in the other cases, complete records of the incident and its resolution are of the utmost importance.

MEDICAL EMERGENCIES

Here we're talking not about accidents but about heart attacks, fainting, strokes, and the like—in other words, emergencies that could have happened anywhere and aren't directly attributable to the restaurant. The way to handle these emergencies isn't really different from the other incidents above—the main difference is that you are probably not at fault and the liability issues are different. Still, the situation must be handled properly, and it is still important to keep complete records of the incident, just in case. Whatever the health situation is, do not hesitate to call 911. Never underestimate the severity of the situation; just call the professionals and let them do their job.

EMPLOYEE EMERGENCIES

THERE ARE SOME FUNDAMENTAL differences between employee emergencies and those that involve guests. One of those differences is that the staff spends quite a few hours every day in potentially hazardous conditions. The other difference is that many of the accidents involving your staff can be prevented through training and diligence—quite a number of injuries among staff members happen because of sheer carelessness.

With regard to hazards, the kitchen is more obviously dangerous than the dining room. Knives, flames, hot pans and sizzler platters, open oven doors, deep fryers, boiling water, hot cooking oil, greasy floors, heavy stockpots, buffalo choppers, food processor blades, and escaping steam are only a few of the dangers to be found in the kitchen. And these all exist in a kitchen where everybody is being careful—imagine when cooks start taking chances or are less careful. I have seen a cook get knocked cold because someone else stacked saucepans incorrectly on an overhead shelf.

Because of the potential for injury in a professional kitchen, it is critical for the staff to know proper first aid, at least for cuts and burns. These are the most common injuries in a kitchen. In fact, for some cooks they are a daily occurrence. This doesn't mean that they shouldn't be taken seriously, though, because a bad infection can lay up one of your cooks for a good while. Make sure that everyone in the kitchen knows basic first aid.

SAFETY PRECAUTIONS IN THE KITCHEN

A safe restaurant starts with a safe kitchen. Just about everybody who works in a food service operation will spend some time in the kitchen, so it pays to train the kitchen staff not to hurt themselves or others. Some of the many areas to cover are as follows:

- **KNIFE HANDLING.** Few things in the restaurant upset me more than sloppy knife handling because it is so easy to avoid. When a staffer walks with a knife, it should be held straight down and against the outside of the leg.

- **HOT PANS.** Anybody carrying equipment that is hot from the stove must announce it to everyone in the vicinity or in their path (to the dish room, the end of the line, or wherever). Commonly used words and phrases are "Hot!" "Hot behind you!" "Slidin'!" and the French "Chaud!" (pronounced "show"), which means "hot."

- **HOT PLATES.** Waiters' hands are usually not toughened like the cooks' are. When putting hot plates up in the window, cooks should warn waiters of a plate that's hotter than usual.

- **JUST WALKING AROUND.** Even when empty-handed, staff should warn people they're walking up behind, because that person might have a knife or hot pan in hand. Kitchens can be pretty tight spaces, and it helps to know when someone is in your vicinity.

- **IN/OUT DOORS.** I have seen people get hurt because someone went in the out door or vice versa. When moving quickly into or out of the kitchen, you should be able to assume that passage through the door is safe—that there isn't someone on the other side of the door either coming toward you or just standing there, either of which can get both of you hurt.

- **WET OR GREASY FLOORS.** Any spill on the kitchen floor can be a danger for the staff. Oil spills in particular are bad, but all spills should be cleaned up quickly. One quick fix for oil is to "sand" the area with kosher salt, which provides some traction. This is, of course, only a temporary remedy, and any spill should be cleaned (and dried) as soon as possible.

The dining room employees are exposed to the kitchen as well as their own side of the house. Thus, they are liable to get hurt in either place. Kitchen injuries are less likely for waiters because they aren't behind the cooking line, where the stoves are, and they spend less time in the kitchen than the cooks do. Dining room injuries can include bad cuts (cutting bread or lemons) as well as bad burns (coffee, bread steamer, heat lamps). Waiters also slip and fall, and they must deal with broken glass more often than cooks, so cuts are quite likely. Many of the hazards for the dining room are the same as those in the kitchen, in particular wet or greasy floors. There are, however, a couple of problems that are more likely to appear in the front of the house.

- **BROKEN GLASS.** Wine and cocktail glasses will fall to the ground and break on occasion. When they do, it's important to clean up the broken glass immediately. As an added precaution, a staff member should stay at the site to warn other staff and guests that there is broken glass on the floor—if not, someone is likely to step right in it and hurt himself or herself. I have noticed that the broken base of a stem glass will often sit sticking straight up, and in that position it can go right through the sole of a shoe.

- **TABLESIDE COOKERY.** Open flames in the dining room? The staff had better be well trained and know where the fire extinguisher is. When waiters are flambéing, make sure they know not to add alcohol to the pan while it's on the rechaud—as noted in Chapter 6, the flame can travel up the stream of alcohol, enter the bottle, and cause an explosion.

- **OTHER FLAMMABLES.** Most restaurants have stopped using unprotected candles on their dining tables; menus can catch fire, as can the napkins used in bread baskets, or even parts of flower arrangements. More than once, I have taken a flaming menu or napkin and stuffed it into the nearest wine bucket to douse the conflagration.

- **THE TRAY OF CHAMPAGNE GLASSES.** Just as every professional cook has carbonized a sheet pan of bacon, every waiter has at some point dumped a tray of full Champagne glasses on a guest. Tulip glasses, when full, have a very high center of gravity and are likely to tip over if the tray is moved quickly, as in when a guest suddenly gestures or moves back in his or her chair. Once the glasses begin to wobble, they are going to fall off the tray, and the only way to save the day is for the waiter to move quickly between the tray and the guests. A waiter's uniform is cheaper to clean than a guest's suede jacket.

- **WINE BOTTLES.** For a while, when the wine industry was switching over from lead capsules to other materials, some wineries were using a metal that, if torn just right, created a razor-sharp edge that could slice your hand open with almost no effort. Another possible hazard is wine bottles that break while being opened. The best way to avoid that is to make sure that both sides of the wine opener's lever are sitting squarely on the lip of the bottle, rather than crooked—undue stress placed on one small spot on the lip can cause a fracture of the glass.

Between the potential for injury in the kitchen and mishaps in the dining room, it's pretty easy to get hurt in our profession. The key, of course, is prevention. The staff should be trained to work in ways that cut down on accidents, and also should know what to do in the inevitable case of something going awry. Fewer calamities, and a staff able to deal with them—it's the best that any of us could hope for.

FACILITY EMERGENCIES

I HAVE SEEN MANY STRANGE THINGS happen to restaurants in the past twenty years—gushing toilets, flooded basements, floods coming from a broken pipe upstairs, fires, blackouts, blizzards, and broken picture windows are only the beginning. When any disaster befalls the facility, the first thing to do is to decide whether or not the restaurant has to be evacuated. The situations that would require such drastic action should be fairly obvious—fires, floods, and other natural disasters among them. There are some occasions, though, when the situation, while troublesome, won't necessarily stop you from serving food. A minor flood in the basement, for instance, might not slow down service at all. Thus, in a less serious circumstance, the decision that has to be made is whether or not service is going to be interrupted. If the answer is yes, the guests have to be alerted with regard to the situation and dealt with in an appropriate manner. If, however, the situation is not bad enough to completely stop service, the guests might still have to hear about it—but maybe just in the form of an apology for the food taking a long time to get to the table. Whatever the situation, decisions have to center around guest and staff safety. You cannot make a decision that will put others in danger, not because of legal issues, but because it is our duty to care for people.

FIRE

We work with open flames on a regular basis. Range tops, tableside flambéing, candles on tables, and the occasional fireplace can be everyday parts of our lives. Luckily for most of us, though, a restaurant fire doesn't occur very often. When a fire does break out in the workplace, do not take chances! Pull the alarm and get everybody out of the building, including yourself. If it's the kind of fire that can be handled with fire extinguishers, all the better, but still evacuate and call the fire department. Do not take chances with this. Also, don't go back into the burning building for anything, no matter how valuable.

If it turns out to have been a false alarm, or if the fire is not very serious and the firefighters allow you and the guests back into the building, the situation switches over from emergency to guest recovery, and you can use steps outlined in the "Guest Recovery" section in Chapter 5.

FLOOD

Whether caused by nature or plumbing, the first thing to do is determine whether the sanitation of the restaurant has been compromised by the inflow of water. A broken water pipe is spewing clean, potable water; a broken toilet, drain line, or sewage pipe is another issue entirely. Also, the severity of the situation should be assessed—particularly hazardous situations are those where the water is in proximity to electrical equipment, hot cooking appliances, or deep fryers. If you see that any of these is a possibility because of a flood, evacuate the kitchen. Turn off equipment if you have time, but get everybody out of there.

SNOWSTORMS

While the interior of the restaurant is probably not affected by severe snowstorms, bad weather can make travel dangerous for staff members and guests. If a particularly bad storm is headed your way, it might make sense to close the restaurant, or at least call both guests with reservations and staffers at home to let them know how bad the weather is likely to get. This doesn't happen very much in urban centers, but suburban and rural locales are subject to some pretty bad driving conditions. The least I will do in this situation is to let the staff members with the longest drives go home early—before the storm hits, if possible.

POWER FAILURES

A power failure is another situation where the safety of your guests and staff determines whether or not you stay open and, if you do, what type of service you will provide. During daylight hours, it's usually a matter of what food and beverage can be served with no power. Also, the computers are down, so all ordering and payment has to be done manually. With regard to safety, the emergency exit signs won't be lit, so it might be against fire regulations to stay open; you should check local laws to find out.

WE HAD A BANQUET FOR 140 starting at six-thirty, and the power went out at four-thirty that afternoon. In the two hours we had to prepare, we pulled the dining room together, collecting votive candles from every nook and cranny, and got ready to move the party along quickly once the guests arrived. The miracle, though, was performed by Chef Dwayne LiPuma and his cooks. They prepared the entire meal with two portable gas burners and our wood-fired oven. Not only was the food as delicious as ever, it was provided in record time. Luckily, it was the second-longest day of the year, so we had daylight until almost nine o'clock. When the lights finally went back on (after dessert had been served), the restaurant staff received a rousing ovation for what they had accomplished. It's evenings like this that make you wonder if there's anything that you can't do.

Once the sun goes down, it gets much harder to stay open. Lighting the room with candles can be romantic but also dangerous. A professional kitchen is dangerous enough with the lights on—with the lights out, it's not worth the risk to your cooks' safety to stay open. One thing about blackouts, though, is that they don't always last long. It might be worth waiting for a little while before shutting down.

RESTAURATEURS AT THEIR BEST

IF YOU GET A few restaurant professionals together and bring up the subject of emergencies, the stories will start coming fast and thick. The common threads that connect most of the restaurant stories, though, are that the restaurant either stayed open or otherwise survived the crisis and that the guests were served dinner as usual, or at least didn't get hurt.

These two themes define the professional restaurateur. First, it is our job to provide the finest food and beverage to our guests no matter what the circumstances. Forget sleet and snow—we'll serve a four-course meal to 140 people during a blackout with nothing more than two rechauds and a wood-burning oven. Second, we care for people. At a certain point, it transcends the earthly bonds of business, and we become caretakers. Yes, it's a job, a profession—we make our livelihood by taking care of strangers. But it is the feeling we get from performing organized acts of kindness that keeps us coming back to our restaurants day after day, meal after meal, guest after guest.

GLOSSARY

BAIN MARIE   Technically a hot-water bath for cooking or holding food, a bain is often used to describe a metal container that sits in the water bath. These containers are used for various purposes in the kitchen, most of which they are not intended for.

BEEFEATER   A popular brand of gin that is particularly good in martinis, as is Bombay gin.

BOH   Back of the house. The kitchen and all operations relating to food preparation.

BOOKING   Taking reservations.

BUFFALO CHOPPER   No, it doesn't chop buffalo. This scary-looking machine consists of a rotating bowl with a set of two vertical spinning blades that chop whatever is going by in the bowl. Its effect is similar to that of a food processor, but it does so in larger quantity.

CLEARING   Removing soiled plates and flatware from a guest's table.

CORKED   Wine that has been tainted by bacteria in the cork that produces TCA (trichloroanisole). Basically, it makes wine smell and taste "musty." Between 3% and 7% of all bottled wines are thought to be thus flawed.

COVERS   The number of people being served.

DEMI-GLACE   A reduced and lightly thickened brown veal stock that is used as the base for many sauces.

DEUCE   A table for two people.

EXPEDITER   Sometimes called the expo. Usually a member of the kitchen staff who coordinates the ordering, firing, and pickup of food from the cooks.

FIRE!   The expediter is telling the cooks to prepare the food to a stage one step away from finished. The call "pick up" means to finish it and send the dish out.

FLATWARE   Silver or stainless steel utensils such as forks, knives, and spoons. Called flat because they can be made from a flat piece of metal.

FOH   Front of the house. The dining room and guest areas.

FOUR-TOP   A table for four; similarly five-top, six-top, and so on.

GRIST   Ground malted grain.

GUERIDON   A small portable table, usually on wheels. Originally the term for a small table used to hold objets d'art, the pedestal of the table being a carved figurine.

HOLLOW WARE   Silver or stainless steel service pieces used to hold and serve liquids. Examples include water pitchers, coffee pots, and soup tureens.

IN THE WEEDS   Also weeded or weeds. So busy that you can't see anything around you; the busier you are, the higher the weeds.

THE LINE   The cooking line in a professional kitchen, usually a row made up of large cooking appliances like ranges, grills, and fryers.

MAITRE D'HÔTEL   Usually shortened to maitre d', its original meaning was general manager, translated as "master of the hotel" or entire establishment. Because the general manager or proprietor was at the front door to welcome guests in many old-school restaurants, the term has devolved to mean "the guy in the tux who brings us to our table."

MALTING	The process of sprouting grain to produce amylase, an enzyme that converts starch to sugar, giving yeast something to eat.
MARKING	A term interchangeable with "resetting" or "mise en placing" the table. Simply, giving each guest the flatware they need for the dish they are about to receive.
ML	Milliliter. A volume measurement used for wine and liquor bottles.
MOD	Manager on Duty.
ORDER!	When the food order goes into the kitchen, the expediter calls out the order to the cooks.
OVERSERVING	Generally used in relation to alcoholic beverages, the term refers to giving a guest more alcohol than he or she should have.
PANTRY	The kitchen area devoted to FOH needs. Usually has storage and refrigeration for dairy and fruit garnishes, as well as coffee and tea products and bread.
PICK UP!	The expediter is telling the cook to finish a dish and send it out.
P&L	Profit & Loss statement. A monthly financial report that reflects the health of your business.
POOLED TIPS	The service staff puts all of their tips into a pool to be shared. Often the size of the share increases with the responsibility of the position.
P.O.S.	Point of sale system. The now ubiquitous computer member of the restaurant staff, used by waiters to send orders to the bar and into the kitchen. It is also used by management to compile sales and inventory reports, and ultimately to fill out financial reports.
PROOF	Two times the percentage of alcohol by volume in a beverage.
PSI	Pounds per square inch. A measurement of pressure.
SIDESTAND	A cabinet in the dining room used to store items needed by the service staff during a meal period.
SIX-PACK	The common package for beer; also used for some expensive or hard-to-get wines that aren't practical to pack in the normal case of twelve bottles.
SLAMMED	When a waiter gets several tables sat at the same time, or when the kitchen gets too many orders at once. Often sends workers into "the weeds."
SOIGNÉ	In French restaurants, this word (pronounced swan-YAY), means just right, smooth and classy. The literal translation is "meticulous" and "well-groomed."
STATION	Work area, either in the kitchen or the dining room.
TURN-AND-BURN	A type of service that focuses on speed, so the patron can serve more guests.
TURNING TABLES	When guests finish and leave their table, allowing for another party to sit there.
WEEDED, WEEDS	See "in the weeds"

RESOURCES

BOOKS

Dale DeGroff. *The Craft of the Cocktail*. New York: Clarkson Potter, 2002.

Harold J. Grossman. *Grossman's Guide to Wines, Spirits, and Beers,* 7th ed., rev. by Harriet Lembeck. New York: John Wiley & Sons, 1983.

Matt Kramer. *Making Sense of Wine*. New York: Morrow, 1989.

Kevin Zraly. *Windows on the World Complete Wine Course*. New York: Sterling Publishing Company, 1988.

PERIODICALS

Cornell Hotel and Restaurant Administration Quarterly. SAGE Publications. Thousand Oaks, CA. (800) 818-7243.

Employment Relations Today. John Wiley & Sons. Hoboken, NJ. (888) 378-2537.

Food Arts. Food Arts Publishing. New York, NY. (212) 684-4224.

Foodservice and Hospitality. Kostuch Publications. Don Mills, Ontario. (416) 447-0880.

Fresh Cup Magazine. Fresh Cup Publishing Co. Portland, OR. (503) 236-2587.

Restaurant Wine. Wine Profits. Napa, CA. (707) 224-4777.

Restaurant Hospitality. Penton Media. Cleveland, OH. (216) 696-7000.

Restaurants and Institutions.
http://www.foodservice411.com/rimag/. (630) 288-8242.

Tea and Coffee Trade Journal. Lockwood Trade Journal Co. New York, NY. (212) 391-2060.

Wine and Spirits. Wine and Spirits Magazine. New York, NY. http://www.wineandspiritsmagazine.com. (212) 695-4660.

Wine Advocate. The Wine Advocate. Monkton, MD. (410) 329-6477.

Workforce Management. Crain Communications. Irvine, CA. http://www.workforce.com.

ONLINE JOURNALS AND WEB RESOURCES

http://www.restaurantreport.com
http://www.opentable.com
http://www.macromedia.com
http://www.kingcocktail.com

ORGANIZATIONS

Federation of Dining Room Professionals (FDRP). Fernandina Beach, FL. http://www.fdrp.com. (877) 264-FDRP.

International Association of Culinary Professionals. Louisville, KY. http://www.iacp.com. (502) 581-9786.

National Restaurant Association. Washington, DC. http://www.restaurant.org. (202) 331-5900.

INDEX

NOTES

NOTES

NOTES

NOTES

NOTES

NOTES